SINGLES

AT THE

CROSS-
ROADS

A Fresh Perspective
on Christian Singleness

Albert Y. Hsu

InterVarsity Press
Downers Grove, Illinois

InterVarsity Press® is the book-publishing division of InterVarsity Christian Fellowship®, a student movement active on campus at hundreds of universities, colleges and schools of nursing in the United States of America, and a member movement of the International Fellowship of Evangelical Students. For information about local and regional activities, write Public Relations Dept., InterVarsity Christian Fellowship, 6400 Schroeder Rd., P.O. Box 7895, Madison, WI 53707-7895.

All Scripture quotations, unless otherwise indicated, are taken from the HOLY BIBLE, NEW INTERNATIONAL VERSION®. NIV®. Copyright ©1973, 1978, 1984 by International Bible Society. Used by permission of Zondervan Publishing House. All rights reserved.

Cover photograph: Bill Aron/Tony Stone Images

ISBN 0-8308-1353-5

Printed in the United States of America ♾

Library of Congress Cataloging-in-Publication Data

Hsu, Albert Y., 1972-
    Singles at the crossroads: a fresh perspective on Christian
singleness/by Albert Y. Hsu.
        p.   cm.
    Includes bibliographical references.
    ISBN 0-8308-1353-5 (alk. paper)
    1. Single people—Religious life.   I. Title.
BV4596.S5H78   1997
248.8'4—dc21   97-26147
                                                                                       CIP

15	14	13	12	11	10	9	8	7	6	5	4	3
10	09	08	07	06	05	04	03	02	01	00	99	

Dedicated to
Kairos,
the single adult community
of Blanchard Road Alliance Church,
Wheaton, Illinois

May we make the most of every opportunity God gives us.

Why This Book?

The average Christian bookstore has more than a hundred titles on marriage and another hundred about parenting, children and family issues. In contrast, these stores stock only about a dozen books about singleness. Half of these are geared for "single-again" divorcees or widows. Of the remainder, most are about "how to find the right one."

The marriage books never argue that marriage is a good thing. That is presupposed. They accept the reality that marriages often have problems, so that's what these marriage books are for: dealing with the problems. But books on singleness usually have a different approach. Instead of dealing with problems that singles might face, these books seem to think singleness *is* the problem. They instruct the reader on how to bide one's time until the right person comes along. In other words, they imply that the solution to the problem of singleness is to get married. Then one can have marriage problems and read all those marriage books.

But is this approach correct? Is singleness the problem? Or does singleness *have* problems, just as marriage has problems? Counselor Gary Collins writes, "It is important to emphasize that singleness in itself is not a problem for all unmarried people. Just as some married people have marriage problems while others do not, so some singles have singleness-related problems that do not bother others."[1]

Furthermore, marriage is not inherently noble. After all, in this fallen world, marriage is the context for some of the most painful social problems and abuses of our modern society. In order to forge a truly Christian marriage, a couple needs a Christian perspective and the redemptive, transforming power of Christ. Just as a man and woman who work at having a Christian marriage can improve their marriage experience, so too can singles with a Christian perspective experience a truly Christian singleness.

I began thinking about the premise of this book when I discovered Rodney Clapp's excellent book *Families at the Crossroads* (Downers Grove, Ill.: InterVarsity Press, 1993). Instead of mere how-to advice for families, this book provided a *theology* of family. It answered the questions, "What does it *mean* to be married? How do we *think* about family and children?"

Furthermore, I was impressed with Clapp's intriguing chapter on "The Superiority of Singleness." Instead of mere methodology about how to find the right one or how to survive being single, what I discovered was a *theology of singleness*—insights and answers to what it *means* to be single. I was challenged to think about Christian singleness in new ways. However, it seemed to me that not many singles would pick up a book titled *Families at the Crossroads* and find that chapter. But what if there was a similar work specifically about singleness? Perhaps—*Singles at the Crossroads?*

I have called this book a "practical theology" of singleness. For singles approaching a complex, postmodern world, I have endeavored to write a work that represents both sound biblical thinking and practical, relevant advice. This book does not presuppose that the only significant crossroads Christian singles come to is the crossroads between singleness and marriage. Rather, I try to grapple with more fundamental issues of Christian identity and search for a biblical, theological and historical context in which to understand being Christian and being single. This work will seek to answer two questions from a Christian point of view: "What does it *mean* to be single?" and "What should the single life *look* like?"

I am indebted to many people for their help in this project. Thanks first to the faculty of the unjustly eliminated communications department of Wheaton College Graduate School, especially my adviser, Dr. Glenn Arnold, as well as Dr. Mark Fackler and Dr. Myrna Grant. Also thanks to Dr. Robert Webber of the Bible/theology department for his thought-provoking and entertaining courses.

Special thanks also to past and present members of the Kairos singles community of Blanchard Road Alliance Church, Wheaton, Illinois, including Lisa Altstadt, Diane Anderson, Jen Dolan, John Estes, Jen Gioffre, Katherine Greenman, Lora Hemminger, Nick Howard, Cheryl Inghram,

Tim Itano, Ryan Jaarsma, Ingrid Korsberg, Lindsey Krogh, Greg Liddle, Julie Lovell, Kristen Mapstone, Rex Martin, Margaret Nagib, Dan Olson, Christian Poland, Hans Riemenschneider, Amy Riniker, Cathy Sevall, Annmarie Turk, Karyn Walker, Char and Matt Wyncoop and many others. I am grateful for the prayers, input, feedback and support of all those who came around me, acted as sounding boards and encouraged me as I developed my thinking. Their help made this book a product of community.

Much appreciation also to my friends and colleagues at InterVarsity Press, many of whom are themselves fine examples of Christian singleness. I am grateful for my editor, Linda Doll, a friend and role model to many. I count it an honor to be part of this publishing house, distinguished in the field for producing thoughtful Christian books.

Special thanks to John R. W. Stott, who graciously took time out of his busy schedule to allow a young graduate student to interview him on the topic of singleness. It is no understatement to say that his ministry via the spoken and written word has instructed and inspired millions. It is a great honor to be able to include his material in this volume.

Also, thanks to friends and faculty at Minnesota Bible College, Rochester, Minnesota, especially Dr. Christopher Davis and Dr. Mark Mangano. More thanks to Dan Stirratt, James Chamberlain, Warren Curry, Dave Karki, Tay Schield, Connie Hanson, Gavin Retzer, Tom Manzke and many others who gave me insights and illustrations. Finally, special thanks to my best friend, Ellen Case, for endless encouragement and support.

May this book help you discover a better understanding of Christian singleness in today's world. "To him who is able to keep you from falling and to present you before his glorious presence without fault and with great joy—to the only God our Savior be glory, majesty, power and authority, through Jesus Christ our Lord, before all ages, now and forevermore! Amen" (Jude 24-25).

1

WHERE SINGLES ARE TODAY

The solitary mortal is certainly luxurious,
probably superstitious, and possibly mad.
SAMUEL JOHNSON

Once upon a time, legend has it, America looked like the small-town, white-picket-fence portraits of Norman Rockwell. Little boys grew up and took up their fathers' professions; little girls aspired to be wives and mothers. The new invention of television depicted happy families where everybody got along, nobody was really bad, nobody ever swore, and Mom and Dad even slept in separate beds. All normal adults were married. All married couples had kids. Nobody got divorced or even talked about it. If you didn't get married soon after high school, something was wrong with you.

This idyllic portrait of America, largely mythical, was shattered by the social upheaval of the sixties and its aftermath. Radical voices challenged all authority and dispensed with the institutions of government, church and marriage. Marriage was declared outmoded and oppressive. Sexual taboos were removed in the name of freedom and liberation.

The ensuing confusion left many Christians fearful of the decay of family, and they yearned for the days before these awful modern times. In reaction, Christians canonized the 1950s suburban nuclear family as traditional, normative and the only legitimate expression of Christian living.[1] The "normal" family consisted of a mother, father, brother and sister.

Thus recent American culture, like most societies around the globe and throughout history, has had little place for singleness—except as a temporary wayside rest in the transition between childhood and marriage. Today's Christian singles, especially, at the end of the twentieth century are at a crossroads, caught between two worlds. Many feel as if they must live up to the expectations of a previous generation where marriage and family were the norm. However, the modern realities of the contemporary culture are much different from the ideals of the past. Let's begin with a glimpse of what singleness in the U.S. looks like today.

The Numbers

More singles overall. A much larger percentage of the population is now single. Throughout the nineteenth and the first half of the twentieth century, less than 5 percent of the U.S. adult population was single.[2] (See figure 1.) However, in the last thirty years the percentage of singles has increased dramatically. In 1996 the U.S. Census Bureau reported that 43 percent of U.S. adults were single: either never married, widowed or divorced. Another 3.5 percent were legally married but separated from their spouses. The remaining 53.5 percent of adults were married and had their spouses present.[3] (See figure 2.) Some experts predict that single adults will account for fully half of the adult population by the turn of the century.[4]

Fewer marriages. A 1991 study reported that the rate at which people were getting married was more than 25 percent lower than in 1960. In 1960, 73.5 marriages took place for every 1,000 unmarried women; in 1991 only 54.2 marriages occurred.[5]

More divorces. The divorce rate has more than doubled in the last three decades. In 1960 nine of every 1,000 married women divorced. By 1991 the number had risen to twenty-one divorces per 1,000 married women.[6] In 1996, as a percentage of the population, 8.9 percent of all American adults were divorced.[7]

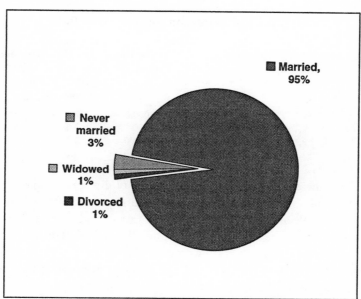

Figure 1. Population of U.S. adults by marital status, 1900

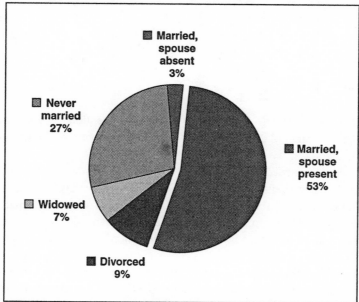

Figure 2. Population of U.S. adults by marital status, March 1996

Marriage and Divorce in America, 1960-90[8]

Year	Number of marriages	Rate of marriages per 1000 population	Number of divorces	Rate of divorces per 1000 population	Divorces per 100 marriages
1960	1,523,000	8.5	393,000	2.2	26
1970	2,158,802	10.6	708,000	3.5	33
1980	2,408,708	10.6	1,182,000	5.2	50
1990	2,448,000	9.8	1,175,000	4.7	48

Note that these numbers are of divorces, not of divorced people. These statistics fail to show what number of marriages are remarriages of divorced people or how many of the divorces are second or third divorces.

Incidentally, it is a common misconception that half of all marriages will end in divorce. J. Allan Petersen writes:

Pollster Louis Harris has written, "The idea that half of American marriages are doomed is one of the most specious pieces of statistical nonsense ever perpetuated in modern times."

It all began when the Census Bureau noted that during one year, there were 2.4 million marriages and 1.2 million divorces. Someone did the math without calculating the 54 million marriages already in existence, and presto, a ridiculous but quotable statistic was born.

Harris concludes, "Only one out of eight marriages will end in divorce. In any single year, only about 2 percent of existing marriages will break up."[9]

While the divorce rate is much less than the conventional wisdom suggests, the number of divorced individuals as an aggregate whole continues to rise gradually.

More never-marrieds. More than one in four American adults have never married. The percentage of singles has been rising steadily over the past several decades. In the 1960s, 15 percent of adults were never-married singles. In 1980, the number had risen to 20 percent. By 1991, the percentage was 23 percent.[10] In 1996, 27.5 percent of the U.S. adult population had never married.[11]

The U.S. Bureau of the Census reports, "Since 1970, the proportions of men and women who had never married have at least doubled and in some cases tripled for the age groups between 25 and 44 years. For example, the proportion of persons 30 to 34 years old who had never married tripled from 6 to 20 percent for women and from 9 to 30 percent for men between 1970 and 1994. Among persons 35 to 39 years old, the proportions never married doubled from 5 to 13 percent for women and tripled from 7 to 19 percent for men, during this period."[12]

The Causes
What are the reasons for this demographic shift? Let's look at several.

Societal change. In the nineteenth century, "religious, social, and economic institutions continued to endorse marriage-and-family ideals. Most people married early, the widowed remarried rather promptly, and divorce was virtually unknown."[13] This began to change at the beginning of the twentieth century as a result of several key events. During the Great Depression and World War II, it became more common for people to remain single and unmarried. Because a large percentage of eligible young men were fighting overseas, both marriage and birth rates were low through 1945.

After the war the baby boom began, and marriage and family came back in vogue. Marriage and birth rates shot up, and the single population stayed low. But by the end of the 1950s, reversals of laws preventing divorce made divorces easier to obtain. By the 1970s, no-fault divorce laws of one form or another had been implemented in all fifty states, allowing people in bad marriages to get out without much legal obstruction.

Throughout the turbulent sixties and seventies, forces such as the hippie movement, the feminist movement and the sexual revolution came into play. Increasing numbers of women attended college and joined the work force. The economy created enough opportunity that women could stand on their own without a husband to provide for them. By 1977, one-third of the American population was single, including those never-married, divorced, separated or widowed.[14]

Postponement of marriage. Not only are fewer people marrying, they are also marrying later. In the last four decades, the average age of people at the time of their first marriage has increased by about four years.

Average Age at First Marriage[15]

Year	Men	Women
1950	22.8	20.3
1960	22.8	20.3
1970	23.2	20.8
1980	24.7	22.0
1990	26.1	23.9
1995	26.9	24.5

Today the median age at first marriage is higher than at any time since 1890, when records were first kept.[16] Why? One reason is young adults have more things they want to do before they get married. Instead of getting married right after high school, going to college is now the norm, and for most, marriage during college is impractical.

In addition, college tends to be prolonged. The bachelor's degree is no longer automatically attained in four years. Many require five, six or more years to complete degrees, due to unavailable classes, changing majors or the need to work in order to afford rising tuition costs. Many students graduate college in their mid to late twenties or early thirties. Also, more students continue schooling beyond the bachelor's level. With a scarcity of good entry-level jobs, more people attend graduate school in hopes of increasing their marketability by having more education on their résumés. Applications to graduate schools, medical schools and law schools are at an all-time high.[17]

Furthermore, many young adults postpone marriage because they have things to do before "settling down." Christian researcher George Barna says, "Many young adults are waiting to get married until their mid-twenties or later because they want to finish their education, pursue a career, or enjoy their freedom. Women, in particular, tend to defer marriage because they are not anxious to shoulder both career and household responsibilities too soon. With the majority of young women leaving school and directly entering the labor force, the woman who marries young and labors as a homemaker is now the aberration."[18]

Fear of divorce. In a groundbreaking 1990 article about "twentysomethings," *Time* magazine reported that this generation of young adults "postpone marriage because they dread divorce."[19] Because the members of Generation X (called "Xers," "baby busters" or "thirteeners")[20] are the sons and daughters of the most-divorced generation in American history, today's young adults are slower to make marriage decisions in hopes of not repeating the mistakes of their parents. They "are not in any rush to get married, hoping that by waiting, time will bring a more compatible mate and the maturity to avoid divorce."[21] Statistics indicate that divorce rates are lower for people who wait to marry. One sociologist concluded, "Divorce rates are lowest for both men and women who marry for the first time at age 28 or later."[22]

While statistics suggest that many of today's young adults will eventually marry, the fact that they are currently postponing marriage means that people are staying single longer. There is a fear of marrying too quickly to somebody who is not "right" for them.

Related to this is "relationship burnout."[23] Many young adults have had painful experiences with relationships, including sexual abuse, date rape, codependency and other dysfunctional situations. Many singles who desire a close relationship find themselves incapable of trust and commitment. "Fear of commitment not only causes some to bail out of perfectly good relationships but others to avoid dating altogether."[24] The general feeling is, "Better not to get too close to anyone; I don't want to get hurt again."

The X factor. Older generations may perceive today's young adults as either being too fickle or afraid of commitment. Though partially true, a more significant factor is the generational shift that Xers have experienced.

First, options have multiplied. A generation ago, television viewers chose between three networks. Today cable TV and satellite dishes provide fifty to more than a hundred networks to choose from. The corner five-and-dime store is a dying breed—now people shop in malls with hundreds of specialty retailers. Instead of just a burger and fries, a food court offers gyros, falafel and dim sum. To keep in touch with a friend, you could use a fax machine, cellular phone, pager or e-mail. No longer are we restricted to snail mail.

Choices apply vocationally as well. Once upon a time a man followed his father's career, and a woman's options were limited to being a teacher or a nurse. No more. The job market has opened almost all professions to both sexes. Barbie no longer has to be the stewardess; she is the pilot. The average university catalog lists hundreds of possible majors.

Given the overwhelming array of options, today's young adults lean toward two extremes. On one hand, they may want to try everything, postponing any final choice because they want to keep their options open. This is why college students often change majors four or five times before settling on something, often by default as graduation looms near.

On the other hand, some are simply overwhelmed by the multitude of choices. Douglas Coupland, author of *Generation X,* defines this phenomenon as "option paralysis": "The tendency, when given unlimited choices, to make none."[25] People withdraw into a reactive, passive mode, hesitant to try anything at all, acquiescing to whatever life dictates. Echoing many in his generation, Keith said, "After graduating from college, I still don't have any more idea of what I want to do with my life than I did when I was a kid."

Leith Anderson, pastor of Wooddale Church in Eden Prairie, Minnesota, states, "They [Xers] seem to be overwhelmed. They cannot decide where to live, what to do, which to choose. They float from one thing to another—jobs, addresses, relationships, convictions. On the other hand, many feel they need to try everything before they decide. Whatever they buy or do, a better product or experience will come along next week or next year. Nothing is permanent. Leave your options open. In six months a better car, computer, or career will come on the market."[26]

Whether consciously or not, many singles approach their dating life the way they choose a major or career—tentatively. Career counselors say that the average person will change jobs at least ten times and entire career tracks may change three or more times, so the wisest thing to do is to keep your options open. This approach shows up in relationships: If I start dating somebody and make a commitment to date that person exclusively, by definition, I have cut myself off from any other possibilities that might be out there. Better not to get too involved with any one person. An upgrade will undoubtedly come along next year.

Other societal trends. Just as a diversified economy has provided alternatives and options for shopping and consumerism, so too have alternatives to traditional marriage become more common in the last forty years. Three of these societal trends are the increase of premarital sex, single parenting and cohabitation.

Society once had the expectation that sexual intercourse was reserved exclusively for one's marital partner. However, changing social mores have resulted in rising statistics of premarital sex and extramarital affairs. Growing societal acceptability of sex outside of marriage has been a disincentive for marriage, since people no longer feel the need to marry in order to have sex. "[In 1970], just under half of all nineteen-year-olds were sexually active; [in 1990], it is nine out of ten. Fewer than one out of every five adults who gets married for the first time these days is a virgin."[27] Virginity now carries the social stigma that adultery and premarital sex once had.

Christians are not immune to these statistics. Various studies have shown that Christians participate in nonmarital sex almost as much as non-Christians. "According to a *Time* survey of frequent church attenders, only 39 percent of those polled thought it was wrong for an unmarried adult to have sex."[28] A study of 1,343 Christian single adults found that 61 percent of the total sample had engaged in sexual intercourse as a single, 52 percent with more than one partner.[29]

Increased premarital sex has led to more children being born to single mothers. Whereas once society ostracized the person who reared a child out of wedlock, such as Hester Prynne in Nathaniel Hawthorne's *The Scarlet Letter,* today such births are tolerated or affirmed as a symbol of independence and self-sufficiency.

In situations of crisis pregnancies, prolife Christians, in particular, encourage unwed teens to bring the child to term instead of aborting it. While many give up their babies for adoption, many others take on the difficult task of single parenting. "Presently there are more than 14 million single-parent families in America. That represents more than one out of every seven families in the nation, an increase of 36 percent since 1970."[30]

One reason for this increase is that an unplanned pregnancy no longer automatically results in marriage. Barna observes that the shotgun wedding has become a relic of the past. He quotes one young mother as saying, "I made one mistake. I'm not gonna multiply it by marrying the guy and ruining what's left of my life."[31]

Cohabitation is also on the rise. The logic of cohabitation, to those who fear divorce, is that if we just live together we won't be married, so if it doesn't work out, we won't have to go through the pain of divorce.

According to the U.S. Bureau of the Census, there were 7 unmarried couples for every 100 married couples in 1994, up from 1 per 100 in

1970—a sevenfold increase. In 1994, 3.7 million unmarried-couple households existed in the U.S. A third of these unmarried couples have children under 15 years of age.[32] According to Barna, "Cohabitation jumped 740 percent between 1970 and 1989, and that growth is showing little evidence of slowing down. From 1987 through 1989, there was an 88 percent increase. Among adults age eighteen to twenty-five, cohabitation skyrocketed by 1,892 percent during that same three-year time span—a twentyfold increase!"[33]

Christians are also increasingly cohabiting. In Koons and Anthony's study, when asked if they had "ever lived with a member of the opposite sex on an intimate, unmarried basis," 22 percent of Christian singles said yes.[34]

Barna concludes, "Since most Americans now accept and even condone premarital sex between consenting adults, the option of having a child without being married . . . and the legality and desirability of cohabitation, much of the pressure to get married young no longer exists."[35]

Expectations Singles Face

The complex changes of the last few decades have resulted in a complex world for today's singles. Singles at a crossroads find pressures and tensions from almost every direction. Here are some of the ways singles are caught between competing expectations.

Self-expectations. Tensions with the single life come first of all from oneself. Most people expect to marry by a particular age, whether it's eighteen, twenty-one, twenty-five or thirty. The expectation is that marriage is a natural development in life's passages: kindergarten, elementary school, junior high, senior high, college, marriage. Many expect to find a mate during college and experience "senior panic" when graduation approaches and no viable candidates for marriage are available.

Libby, a character in a novel by Minnesota author Jon Hassler, felt this way:

> She hated hearing about people who never got themselves matched up with anybody, and that was why at sixteen she'd already had seven or eight boyfriends and would have as many more as it took to find the right one to marry. Despite the unhappy example of her parents, the single life was her idea of hell on earth.[36]

During the course of the novel, Libby cycles through three unhappy marriages. Ironically, the abuse and destructiveness she experiences in her marriages are probably far more hellish than if she had remained single. Nevertheless, many singles share Libby's belief that singleness is "hell on earth."

Family expectations. Perhaps the greatest source of singles' discomfort about their identity comes from their parents and family. I received this e-mail message from Connie, a twenty-two-year-old college senior:

> Hey Al!! How was your Christmas? My Christmas was okay. I found out that another one of my cousins is getting married this summer. He is the same age as me and now my great grandma and other people in my family basically treat me like crap because I don't have a boyfriend and I am not getting married soon. It is almost like I am not a person if I don't have a boyfriend. Grr. My brother told me that I must be a pretty big loser to have chased Steve away. I just can't believe the pressure that they put on me. Unfortunately, I came back from Christmas and now I have an ulcer. I know that must be a terribly big shock (yeah, right) but I am dealing with it. Well, I better go. I just wanted to say hi! Catch ya later! Love, Conn

Two cousins on one branch of Connie's family were getting married the next summer, but none of the grandchildren in her particular branch were engaged. Being of "marrying age," Connie felt the pressure to be the next in line in her family to marry. But Connie had recently broken up with her boyfriend of three years, so marriage was not a likely prospect in the near future. The message that Connie received from her family was that it's not acceptable to be single.

These family pressures show up in different ways. The oldest child may feel pressured to find a spouse if a younger sibling gets engaged first. Or the youngest child may feel pressured if all the older siblings are married. An only child may feel pressure to marry and have children to continue the family line, especially if there are not other cousins to preserve the family name. One single said that he feels pressure to marry from relatives because his older brother is gay. Since his brother has "opted for the non-marriage route," he is next in line to marry.

Parents may give married children preferential treatment over single children. Diane, twenty-eight, has three siblings, all of whom are married. At Christmas, her parents give her siblings Christmas gifts that are meant for couples. One year, "they all got boxes of steaks," Diane said. "But my gift was different. I got spark plugs for my car."

Social pressures. Most singles know how it feels when it seems like all of one's closest friends are getting married. With each passing wedding, more friends leave the single life and join the married people's world. In circles where marriage seems to be the rite of passage into adulthood, singles are perceived as developmentally challenged.

A common difficulty is the problem of interacting with married friends. Most singles have experienced the feeling of being a "third wheel." An additional pressure occurs when well-meaning married people take it upon themselves to play matchmaker for their single friends. The comic strip character Cathy experiences this. When a married friend tries to set Cathy up with somebody entirely incompatible with her, saying, "You're both still single! It's perfect! You're both still single!" Cathy thinks to herself, "Everyone feels obligated to make a sandwich out of the last two slices of bread."[37]

Walter, a twenty-four-year-old, said, "My pastor is always trying to match me up with someone else in the church, even if she's thirty-three years old and not my type." Often such match-ups are doomed from the start and only serve to aggravate one's feeling of non-marriedness. The unspoken but underlying message may be that singles are not complete without a spouse.

Sometimes well-intentioned but insensitive married people ask singles, "Are you still single?" Some annoyed singles might feel like responding, "Yes, I am. Are you still married?" One single said, "It's so rude when they ask me, 'How's your love life?' Maybe I should ask them, 'How's your sex life?'"

Church expectations. Since birth, Becky has been attending the same home church, a small congregation of about 150. She attended a Christian college and got engaged, and the older members of her church approved. "Our little Becky is getting married," they said happily.

"But I broke the engagement," Becky said. "Nobody I knew ever did that. I thought I was weird." People in her church were mortified. She remembers the feelings of pity she received. "It was like, 'She's out of her Christian college, she had a Christian man. Where's she going to find a Christian man now? She missed her chance. Now she has to go into the world and find a man. . . .'"

In Becky's church, most women of her age had gotten married after high school or two years of college. "But I was going to get my master's and I was focusing on my career instead of becoming a mom. By choosing a career instead of getting married, I kind of got labeled a feminist."

Though single adults comprise nearly half of the population, this is not reflected in the population of most local churches. "According to national surveys, in most churches, the single population is 15 percent. And the smaller the church, the less population of single people there are, because of this real focus on family and nothing else—family defined as one man, one woman, three children and a dog."[38]

Many singles have felt out of place at churches. One single man was very turned off by the compartmentalizing of singles in the church. "Before I was just a Christian and now I'm a single," he said. "In one church the first thing they did was give me a little survey. 'Are you single?' Boom! They knew exactly where to send me and I did not want to go there! It was the opposite of what I was looking for. I want to go to church and be part of the body, not part of a database."

Regional differences. It can be more acceptable to be single in some parts of the country than in others. The single population in major metropolitan areas is much higher than in rural areas. For example, New York City has a single population of 58 percent. Los Angeles is 54 percent single. Singles who live in rural areas may not have many other available single adults to date and marry.

One student who came to a Midwestern university from the East Coast was surprised that "it seems like out here everybody expects to get married right after college." That was not the case where she grew up. On the other hand, another woman felt that there was less pressure to marry in the Midwest than in her native South. "In the South, there's more expectations and pressure for a woman to get married," she said.

Ethnic expectations. The sons and daughters of first-generation immigrants often have an additional struggle. Not only must they contend with the expectations of contemporary American culture, but also they must grapple with the cultural expectations and traditions of their parents and families. For example, Asian cultures expect women to be obedient to their fathers when unmarried, obedient to their husbands when married and obedient to their sons when widowed. The cultural emphasis on the woman's place being in the home and raising a family is an additional pressure for young single women.

A bright Asian-American female completing her Ph.D. shares that she still feels the effect of her parents' disappointment as they express their concern about her single status at thirty-five years of age. Even with her professional competence, they tell her that they feel that she will not be cared for unless she marries. Further, at her age, the unlikelihood that she will bear children makes her a poor marriage candidate. Thus, a very capable Asian woman has to deal with the psychological threat of inadequacy because she may not carry out her traditional "place" as wife and mother.[39]

Furthermore, singles may find that they are not accepted as full adults in other cultural contexts. Many cultures consider anybody who is not married to be a "youth," regardless of age. Thus, when single missionaries enter other cultures, they discover that their witness is less credible than if they were married, because they are considered to be only a boy or a girl, not yet a man or woman.

Gender differences. "I think it's different for men and women," one woman observed. "A man can be a thirty-year-old single and nobody is, like, freaking out. But for a woman . . ."

Sociologist Deborah Tannen suggests, "Though all humans need both intimacy and independence, women tend to focus on the first and men on the second."[40] The need for intimacy may propel women into a search for relationship, believing that they need to have a man to be fully human.

Men and women also face different stereotypes. Women face the image of the old maid or the spinster. Single women may worry that they will be perceived as too independent or domineering to have close relationships. As one novelist's single-female protagonist said, "Of course, there's still this idea that single women are supposed to feel barren, literally and figuratively. Especially if they compound their misery by being successful."[41]

Author Barbara Holland reflects,

For ages past, women were defined only in relation to other people, and the definition lingers; a woman may be called a wife and mother for most of her life, while a man is called a husband and father only at his funeral. Even today a solitary woman may feel like the tree falling in the empty forest; alone in a room, nobody's daughter, wife, lover, mother or executive assistant, her ectoplasm thins out until the furniture shows through. Let someone else walk in and she solidifies in relation to the visitor, but alone her outlines fade.[42]

Unmarried men are often viewed as uncommitted or selfish, too wrapped up in their own concerns to settle down and get married. Friends may quietly wonder if they are gay. Single men may also face fears that they could be perceived as child molesters, sex offenders or some other criminal element. One single youth pastor said, "I fear that someone's going to worry if I invite kids from the youth group over to my apartment. Everybody knows me really well, but still I wonder if that could look weird."

Biological considerations. Tay is the director of admissions at a small Christian college. She has a fruitful ministry, travels extensively, spending four or five months on the road every year, including ten weeks every summer at senior high youth camps and conferences. She has been on trips to Alaska, New Zealand and Israel. She loves leading worship and doing youth ministry. But one thing about being single nags at her.

"I turn thirty this year," Tay said. "Inside, I'm physically changing. I think some hormonal changes are happening. Until this last year I've never yearned to have a kid. But now . . . where did that yearning come from? I've never thought about them before. But now that I'm turning thirty, I feel like I do want to have a kid someday."

More so for women than men, but nevertheless for all singles as they get older, there is a recognition that the biological clock is ticking. Women who want to bear children worry that they may never have the chance.

In the 1989 movie *When Harry Met Sally,* Sally laments, "I'm almost forty!"

"In seven years!" says Harry.

"But someday!" cries Sally. As singles enter the thirties and forties, they have a growing feeling that time is running out.

Some singles find that at certain ages it becomes less acceptable to have never married. One man described his brother's situation. Forty and never married, he didn't fit into his church's singles group, which was primarily twentysomethings fresh out of college. "If he was divorced, that would be fine. He'd have a class to go to. But forties-and-never-married didn't fit anywhere."

Other issues. Lora finds "buy one, get one free" offers at grocery stores biased against singles. "I'm only cooking for one," she said. "Why do I need to stock up?"

Sometimes it may seem to the single that everything in society is geared toward couples and families. "There is no arguing that we still live in a couples-oriented society (although that emphasis is fading)," Koons and Anthony write. "Restaurant seating is geared for couples, food is usually packaged for two or more people, and products for a twosome lifestyle are marketed in our media. Books, magazines, radio and television continue to sell singles the message that if you want to fit in with the mainstream of society, you need to be paired up."[43]

The Different Faces of Singleness

Examples of singleness vary widely. At one end of the spectrum is the role model of the saintly Mother Teresa, who has spent her entire life as a single woman ministering sacrificially to the poor of Calcutta. At the other extreme might be Theodore Kazcynski, the alleged Unabomber, a lonely, isolated single man who was unable to build relationships with people, who wrote to his parents about his desperate longing to marry, who withdrew from society and allegedly terrorized and killed innocent people. Both are single, but what a stark contrast.

Stereotypes of singles are constantly in flux. In the sixties and seventies, much was said of "swinging singles" and the promiscuous single lifestyle. In the eighties, the media projected the image of the yuppie—the professional single parent who competently handled both career and parenting. In the nineties, the picture shifted yet again to the young Xer singles who spend all their time hanging out in a coffeehouse.

We must recognize that there is no such thing as a "typical" single, any more than there is a "typical" marriage. Every single adult has personal circumstances and situations that prevent him or her from being neatly pigeonholed. Traditionally, singles have been categorized in the three groups of "never-married," "divorced" and "widowed," but these general categories do not adequately describe the differences between singles within each group.

Others categorize singles as either *volitional* singles (those who are single by choice and wish to remain so) or *nonvolitional* singles (those who have not consciously made any decision to remain single). But even here there are distinctions. Here are some other possible identifications.

The most easily identifiable singles are what may be called *vocational* singles. These individuals' occupation in life requires them to be unmarried. These include Catholic priests and nuns who have taken vows of celibacy and chastity as part of their religious vocation. Other vocational singles include Protestant missionaries who have chosen the single life in order to better accomplish their work. A related category could be called *professional* singles. Though not necessarily single by choice, these hardworking careerists may find themselves so consumed by their work that they are essentially married to their job and have no time for dating or marriage.

Others are *ideological* singles. Some, for purposes of political statement or because of a philosophy of belief, choose to remain single. Someone crusading against global overpopulation might remain single in order not to contribute to the problem. Or somebody may view marriage as an outdated, oppressive institution that restricts personal freedom. In an interview with David Letterman, television personality Roseanne said, "I don't like the institution of marriage. I don't think it's good for women. And I don't think any woman should ever get married."[44] A woman who has been victimized and abused by men throughout her whole life may be unwilling to get into relationships.

There are also *biological* singles—those who, for whatever reason, have no desire or capacity for heterosexual marriage. Some people have hormonal differences that result in their being completely uninterested in relationships with members of the opposite sex. Or "chronic illness and handicaps, both physical and mental, [can] reduce the person's potential for marriage and could hinder a satisfying relationship with someone of the opposite sex."[45] Others are homosexual in orientation, whether by nature or nurture, genetics or personal choice, and this may prevent or discourage them from entering heterosexual marriage.

A significant phenomenon today are *single-again* singles. This includes widows/widowers and divorcees. In this age of no-fault divorce, some of these singles have become single again against their will. Others have initiated the divorce or separation from the former spouse. This means that different single-agains will view their return to singleness differently. For some, being single again is a state of abandonment, rejection and loss. For others, it is freedom from an abusive situation and a chance to start again. Just as there is no typical single, there is no typical divorcee or widower either.

Yet another group are *virtual* singles—people who are married or in a serious relationship but for whatever reason are not able to be physically present with their partners. Though married or committed, they still function as singles. This is especially common in military marriages, where one partner may be stationed far from the other. Or one's career may require extensive travel. A medical student might serve a residency in a hospital far away from her spouse. Though these people have a significant other, their daily life is mostly lived as single adults.

The opposite situation could be called *married* singles. Though technically unmarried, these singles cohabit with a short- or long-term boyfriend or girlfriend, sharing an apartment or house together as if married. Sometimes two divorced people live together without official remarriage and blend their families. Or people may establish "marriage alternatives" such as homosexual domestic partnerships.

Another subgroup of married singles are engaged couples who, though not yet officially married, have begun the process of combining their lives. For these individuals, the attitude and approach to life has already become that of the corporate identity of a married couple. This is especially noticeable when an engaged person speaks in the plural, "Oh, we have that CD," even when they are not officially married yet. They think in terms of the future "Mr. and Mrs." and no longer consider themselves as single. Thus, a broken engagement or death of a fiancé can be devastating. Not only must they grieve the loss of the partner, but they also experience the difficulty of shifting back to a single person's worldview.

Perhaps most common of all are those who do not fit any of the previous categories. Most of these singles view themselves as *temporary* or *transitional* singles. Never married, fully expecting to marry someday, these singles view singleness as a phase of life that comes between adolescence and marriage. Some are actively looking for a marriage partner but haven't found the right person yet. Others may have plenty of options, but they are not yet ready to settle down. Attitudes in this group may range from an idealistic "Someday my prince(ess) will come" to a pessimistic "All the good ones are taken."

"There are two types of singles," Bob observed. "There are the ones who aren't worried about it, who date but just haven't gotten married yet, and there are the older ones who are starting to wonder."

Another single said, "You go from thinking 'This is temporary' to 'I wonder if this is temporary . . .'"

Some of these people fall into the category of *disillusioned* singles. They have unwillingly resigned themselves to the single life and are characterized by a hopeless or bitter spirit and feelings of despair and defeat. They may view their singleness as a punishment for some wrong they have committed, or they may raise a fist in anger against the powers that be, blaming God for inflicting an undesirable state upon them. Some see themselves as victims of fate. Others may just passively accept their lot in life as God's will.

Is there an alternative to all this? Can Christian singles find a positive view of singleness that moves beyond traditional expectations and stereotypes? However one might classify or categorize today's singles, several things are clear. One is that singleness itself does not determine a particular lifestyle. Singleness in and of itself does not make one into either Mother Teresa or the Unabomber. More significant is our attitude toward being single and how we choose to live as singles.

To that end, singles at the crossroads are asking many questions. "Am I to be single forever, or will I eventually marry?" "What is God's will for my life as a single?" "How do I satisfy my needs for companionship and relationship?" "What is my identity in a world of married couples?"

This book will attempt to find answers to some of these questions and set forth a new vision of singleness for the twenty-first century. In order to lay a foundation for this task, we will begin by answering a crucial question: "What does God think of singles?" The next few chapters will explore this issue.

Discussion Questions

1. How do you feel singles are stereotyped in today's culture? Has this changed during your lifetime?
2. Were you surprised to read that such a large percentage of the population is single? Does it seem that way to you?
3. What expectations have been imposed on you as a single? How have you responded to them?
4. How do you view yourself as a single? Do you fit into any of the categories suggested?

2

A BRIEF HISTORY OF SINGLENESS

I praise matrimony. But only because it produces virgins.
JEROME

Jerome, a Christian leader of the fourth century, compared the states of virginity, widowhood and marriage by making an allusion to the parable of the sower (Mt 13:8). He gave virginity a numerical value of one hundred, widowhood sixty, and marriage thirty.[1] In fact, Jerome "went so far as to say that he saw no reason for Christians to have children of their own—pagans would produce sufficient offspring as raw material for spiritual rebirth!"[2] This may sound strange to modern ears since our present-day society, even with all its changes, still recognizes marriage and family as normative over singleness.

Let's look at how Christians have thought about singleness over the centuries and how this can help us in our modern-day attempt to understand singleness.

The Old Testament: Jewish Background

To understand how Christians have viewed singleness, we must begin with Christianity's Jewish roots. The Old Testament Israelite community, like most of the ancient world, was based on family clans and stressed the importance of marriage and children. "The Old Testament provides no real place for single people," Rodney Clapp writes. "Even ascetics such as the priests and the Nazirites were not single (Lev 21:1-15; Num 6:1-21). In fact, for a Hebrew not getting married was catastrophic."[3] To be without spouse and children was to be without inheritors and guardians in old age. In Jewish society, marriage was the norm. Children were seen as blessings and were expected of every married couple.

One key reason for this was the lack of certainty about an afterlife. Whereas Christians can place their hope in the resurrection of the body, Old Testament Jews could only be assured of descending into Sheol—the grave. Therefore, "for the Hebrews, survival after death was primarily a matter of handing on the family name, especially through the eldest son."[4] This is partly why the Old Testament stresses family lineages and genealogies. The curse of being single was not that one could not participate in sex but that one would not have children to continue the family line.

In fact, this is part of the reasoning behind the instruction of Deuteronomy 24:5: "If a man has recently married, he must not be sent to war or have any other duty laid on him. For one year he is to be free to stay at home and bring happiness to the wife he has married." This was not only to enhance the new marriage but, most significantly, to produce an heir. The battlefield death of a new husband who had not yet fathered children often meant familial extinction. This law was written to help ensure that men would beget sons who would carry their name.

Because of this, barrenness was dreadful in the Old Testament. Genesis 16 describes how Sarah was unable to conceive an heir for Abraham and so provided the use of her handmaid Hagar to produce Ishmael. The following generation also encountered barrenness. "Isaac prayed to the Lord on behalf of his wife, because she was barren. The Lord answered his prayer, and his wife Rebekah became pregnant" (Gen 25:21). In the narrative of Jacob and his wives, Rachel was jealous of Leah's ability to bear children. She was so distraught that she said to Jacob, "Give me children, or I'll die!" (Gen 30:1).

The Mosaic law promised that if the Israelites were obedient, "the fruit of your womb [would] be blessed" (Deut 28:4). Both barrenness and lifetime singleness were seen as curses. In the book of Judges, Jephthah's daughter "went into the hills and wept because she would never marry" (Judg 11:38). "We see . . . in the lamentation of the daughter of Jephthah, that virginity was regarded almost as a disgrace, and that childbearing was considered the noblest function of woman."[5] Isaiah prophesied that at the time of God's judgment, "seven women will take hold of one man and say, 'We will eat our own food and provide our own clothes; only let us be called by your name. Take away our disgrace!'" (Is 4:1).

Only rarely did unmarried people play a role in Old Testament history. These exceptions include some of the prophets, such as Elijah and Elisha. Daniel may have been a eunuch in Babylon. Jeremiah was commanded by God, "You must not marry and have sons or daughters in this place" (Jer 16:2), as part of his prophetic testimony. Though used mightily by God, these singles did not enjoy the affirmation of Jewish society. Rather, they were viewed as eccentric, ascetic anomalies.

While the Israelite nation had no real place for the unmarried, this did not mean that they were forgotten by God. God promised to remember the singles who were faithful to him.

"Sing, O barren woman,
    you who never bore a child;
burst into song, shout for joy,
    you who were never in labor;
because more are the children of the desolate woman
    than of her who has a husband," says the Lord. . . .
Let not any eunuch complain,
    "I am only a dry tree."
For this is what the Lord says:
"To the eunuchs who keep my Sabbaths,
    who choose what pleases me
    and hold fast to my covenant—
to them I will give within my temple and its walls
    a memorial and a name
    better than sons and daughters;
I will give them an everlasting name
    that will not be cut off." (Is 54:1-2; 56:3-5)

God's promise to the single and childless is that their memory will not be forgotten.

Jewish attitudes against celibacy were even more strict by the time of the New Testament. According to the rabbinical teaching of the Mishnah, Jewish men were required to be married and beget children. "Any man who has no wife is no proper man," taught one rabbi.[6] Others suggested that God watches to see when a man will marry, and "as soon as one attains twenty and has not married, He exclaims, 'Blasted be his bones!'"[7] In Jewish society, it was simply unthinkable that anyone, let alone a religious leader, would not be married.

The New Testament: Christian Teaching

Jesus came into this Jewish culture and shattered all their prejudices. In sharp contrast to Jewish conventional wisdom, Jesus taught that salvation is not found in marriage and that eternal life does not come from having sons to carry the family name. Rather, salvation and eternal life are found in following Jesus. Dignity and personhood come not from marriage and progeny but from identity within the kingdom of God.

Jesus also taught that marriage is not an eternal state. In Matthew 22:30 Jesus said, "At the resurrection people will neither marry nor be given in marriage; they will be like the angels in heaven." Jesus points out that marriage is an institution of this worldly sphere and is unnecessary in the kingdom of heaven. Therefore, followers of Jesus should not place their hope and trust in the institutions of marriage and family. Marriage and offspring are no guarantee of everlasting life, contrary to Jewish belief. Only the resurrection carries eternal significance.[8]

While the biological family is ultimately temporary in nature, Jesus created in his disciples a new family—the church—that would endure for eternity. Therefore allegiance to Christ has priority over familial ties. When Jesus' mother and brothers came looking for him, he pointed at his disciples and said, "Here are my mother and my brothers. For whoever does the will of my Father in heaven is my brother and sister and mother" (Mt 12:49-50). His coming would set children against their parents, he said, "and one's foes will be members of one's own household. Whoever loves father or mother more than me is not worthy of me; and whoever loves son or daughter more than me is not worthy of me" (Mt 10:35-37 NRSV).

In fact, Jesus' message was so radical that following him could even come between husband and wife. Jesus said that those who had left their houses or parents or children—or their wives—for the sake of the kingdom of God would receive much blessing (Lk 18:29). While Jesus was not advocating abandonment of marriage and family responsibilities, he made it clear that following him was more important than even the dearest of human relationships. This new priority gives new value to the single person.

In his teaching on marriage and divorce, Jesus said that some had "made themselves eunuchs for the sake of the kingdom of heaven" (Mt 19:12 NRSV). To understand the significance of this statement, we must understand the role of the eunuch in ancient civilizations.

Because of their physical condition, eunuchs were not capable of having children. It was thought that this especially qualified them to serve in positions of authority and government because they could attend to their duties without the distraction of family concerns and presumably without the risk of sexual temptation. For example, the book of Esther mentions seven eunuchs who served the Persian king Xerxes (1:10) and other eunuchs who attended Queen Esther (4:4). One of the king's eunuchs was "in charge of the women" (2:3), another "in charge of the concubines" (2:14), and another "in charge of the harem" (2:15). The Ethiopian eunuch of Acts 8 was similarly a government official in charge of the treasury of Candace, queen of the Ethiopians (v. 27).

One reason that eunuchs were especially valuable to kings was that such rulers were very concerned about the succession to their thrones. Kings feared that others would usurp their authority and claim kingship for themselves and their offspring. Eunuchs, who had no children, were thought to pose no such threat. "For a king jealous of his authority and fearful for his throne, a man necessarily without dynastic ambitions was a great help."[9] Thus the eunuchs' physical state of perpetual celibacy provided them the opportunity to serve their king with wholehearted devotion and loyalty.

Against this background, the significance of Jesus' teaching in Matthew 19 is that it affirms that *single persons are no less whole people for lack of marriage,* in contrast to Jewish thought. Rather, both married and unmarried people are equally able to serve God. Those who have "renounced marriage because of the kingdom" (v. 12 NIV) are honored as complete individuals who have chosen a life of selfless service and devotion to Christ their King.

While affirming both singleness and marriage as good gifts from God, the apostle Paul noted that there were certain practical advantages for the unmarried. "Those who marry will face many troubles in this life, and I want to spare you this," Paul wrote (1 Cor 7:28). An unmarried person was "free from concern" and able to be "concerned about the Lord's affairs" without having his or her interests divided (1 Cor 7:32-34). Though he was strongly committed to the institution of marriage and counseled married persons to remain in their marriages, Paul was so convinced of the advantages of singleness that he wished more singles would choose to remain unmarried.

Compared to the Jewish attitudes of the first century, Jesus and Paul were truly revolutionary. Their very lives as single adults provided role models for Christians who may have never seen an unmarried religious leader before. Theologian Stanley Grenz says of John the Baptist, Jesus and Paul,

> In none of these cases does the New Testament elevate the single status as being the fulfillment of the person's divine vocation, nor is singleness affirmed on the basis of an ascetic rejection of marriage. What is significant is that each of these individuals as a single person carried out a God-given mission within the divine economy, indicating thereby that one need not be married to serve God.[10]

Without demeaning marriage, the New Testament gives a new dignity to singleness. Both states are equally valid ways to serve God. After all, Peter was married (1 Cor 9:5); Paul was not. Both were used mightily to further the kingdom of God.

In sum, "the Christian perspective on the biblical material is that, while the first created human beings, Adam and Eve, were a married couple, in the new creation the second Adam, Jesus Christ, was a single person. Singleness and marriage are parallel routes for loving and serving in the world and preparing for life in the resurrection community."[11]

The Early Church: Orthodoxy and Heresy

In the second and third centuries, most early church leaders followed Paul in commending the celibate life. Ignatius noted that abstinence from marriage for the purpose of honoring God was not uncommon; he instructed that it should be wholly voluntary and conducted with humility and secrecy. Justin Martyr and Origen similarly commended celibacy when it sprang from a desire to serve God.[12]

In fact, tradition says of Origen that "in his youthful zeal for ascetic holiness, he even committed the act of self-emasculation, partly to fulfill literally the mysterious words of Christ in Matthew 19:12 [there are eunuchs who have made themselves eunuchs] for the sake of the kingdom of God, partly to secure himself against all temptation and calumny which might arise from his intercourse with many female catechumens."[13]

In the early church, singleness was viewed as a truly freeing and liberating opportunity. A young Christian in the second century would have heard an onslaught of family-values rhetoric—coming not from the Christian community but from pagan sources. In ancient Greco-Roman culture, marriage and procreation were seen as civic duties. All good citizens were pressured to be productive members of society, in the literal sense of providing many offspring who would become craftsmen and soldiers to fill roles necessary for the functioning of civilized society. Furthermore, arranged marriages were still common. Children were expected to marry well and continue the family's name and prestige.

In classical Greek and Roman society, a young man or woman who hesitated or refused to marry the person chosen by his or her family would be considered insubordinate or possibly even insane. Many parents expected their daughters to marry at about the age of puberty or soon after; in aristocratic circles, advantageous marriages sometimes were arranged when the children were as young as six or seven. Through marriage, as the historian Peter Brown says, "a girl was conscripted as a fully productive member by her society, as was her spouse." Young men were expected to marry between the ages of seventeen and twenty-five and then to place themselves at the service of their communities, according to their family tradition and station.[14]

Christian singleness offered an alternative to this. "As surprising as it may seem to us, it was the church that provided an escape from the pressure to marry and reproduce."[15] In contrast to parental and family-arranged marriages or marriage as a civic duty, the Christian single was able to proclaim that allegiance to Christ was more important than even the bonds of family or state. The first priority was to serve Christ and his church. Any obligations to the biological family came second.

Furthermore, the pressing issues of the early days of the church, such as threats of persecution and martyrdom, provided other reasons for Christians to remain celibate. "The call to martyrdom outweighed all other calls. If put to the test, the mother would be called to forsake her nursing child; the father would have to abandon a whole household of dependents. Familial ties were precious, but the Christian's paramount allegiance was, without question, to God."[16]

Whereas early Christians practiced celibacy on a voluntary basis for the purpose of more effective ministry, the heretical Gnostics encouraged celibacy because of their belief that the body was evil. While there are hints of Gnostic thought in the New Testament, such as those in Corinth who wanted to abstain from sex even in marriage (1 Cor 7:3-5), a fully developed Gnostic theology did not arise until the second and third centuries.

The basic Gnostic worldview was a dualism of two worlds, one of spirit and one of matter. They believed that only spiritual things could be good and holy, while everything physical was evil and corrupt. Therefore God could only exist as spirit, not as a human body. The Incarnation was thus impossible—God coming into human form through human childbirth was a disgusting concept. Gnostics believed that human beings were good spirits trapped in evil bodies of flesh.

The Gnostic view of matter as evil had direct application to issues of the body and marital relationships. The implications of their theology led to two expressions. Some fell into a form of libertarianism, reasoning that physical flesh was of this world and therefore could not affect their spiritual souls. These Gnostics, claiming the unimportance of the physical body, felt free to indulge in all manner of physical and sexual experiences. Some even believed that souls needed to participate in every imaginable physical expression before they could encounter God.

Other Gnostics entered into asceticism. Since they believed the body was evil, they took every measure possible to deny all physical pleasures and urges, sometimes practicing extreme forms of self-mortification. Some fled to deserts to escape the evils of society. Some ran away from women as if fleeing demons. Most viewed marriage as a deadly sin, an evil participation in the world of matter. In his treatise *Against Heresies,* Irenaeus in A.D. 180 wrote against the Gnostic Saturninus and his followers, who claimed that "to marry and procreate . . . is of Satan."[17]

These two Gnostic approaches, libertarianism and asceticism, confronted Christianity in the early centuries of the church. Orthodox Christians responded to these heretical Gnostic philosophies by defending the Incarnation and affirming Jesus' humanity and divinity. The church sought to distance itself from libertarian licentiousness and called for a return to holiness and purity.

However, Christians did not come away from their interaction with the Gnostics unscathed. In reacting against the libertarians, many Christians swung the pendulum too far and embraced asceticism. Against the evils of the day, asceticism was an attractive alternative that squared well with what Paul had taught about the advantages of singleness.

Church historian Rebecca Harden Weaver suggests that while Christians rightly refuted the dualism of the Gnostics, they still were products of their age and expressed a certain ambivalence toward the body. For example, in the third century Clement of Alexandria affirmed the necessity of marriage, "both for the sake of our country and for the succession of children and for the completion of the world. . . . Since God has so ordered the world as to make procreation essential, sexual intercourse is to be understood as part of our obedience to God and our debt to the human community."

However, Clement qualified these remarks by saying, "Even so, there are clear boundaries on such behavior. To have intercourse without intending children is to violate nature. . . . Marriage is the desire for procreation, but it is not the random, illicit or irrational scattering of seed. Sexual activity is to be limited to marriage, is to be engaged in solely for the sake of procreation, and is to be undertaken as a purposeful, reverent endeavor."[18]

Though Clement wanted to affirm marriage as an institution created and ordained by God, he viewed human sexuality as a necessary evil. In this we see a hint of how Gnostic asceticism influenced Christian theology of the body. Christians believed they were not to indulge in sexual intercourse for fear of giving in to the evils of the flesh.

Jerome, likewise, declared that Jesus remained "a virgin in the flesh and a monogamist in the spirit," faithful to his only bride, the church. Writing against Jovinian, who was condemned as a heretic, Jerome wrote, "He puts marriage on a level with virginity, while I make it inferior; he declares that there is little or no difference between the two states; I claim that there is a great deal." Jerome went on to boldly state, "I will say what the apostle [Paul] has taught me. . . . indeed in view of the purity of the body of Christ, all sexual intercourse is unclean."[19]

This idea is furthered in the thinking of later theologians such as Augustine. Before his conversion, Augustine spent his young adult years as a notorious womanizer. In his quest for meaning, he spent nine years with the Gnostic Manichaeans, who encouraged asceticism and taught that the material world was evil. Though he later converted to a more orthodox form of Christianity, it is possible that those years as a student of Manichaean philosophy influenced his views on human sexuality. He believed that sin was transmitted from generation to generation through the act of sexual intercourse. Like Clement, Augustine said that intercourse should be practiced only for the purpose of procreation and should not be enjoyed. While begetting and rearing children were "duties," Augustine said that "virginal integrity and freedom from all carnal relations through holy chastity is an angelic lot, and a foretaste in the corruptible flesh of perpetual incorruption. . . . Fertility is a blessing in marriage, but [virginal] integrity in holiness is better."[20]

This more clearly articulated theology of celibacy directly impacted the priesthood. In the early days of the church, most leaders were married. Paul counseled that elders must be husbands to only one wife (1 Tim 3:2), condemning polygamy but permitting marriage. However, Gnostic influence caused an increasing movement toward asceticism. Throughout the second and third centuries many priests and bishops chose to be unmarried.

During these centuries, persecution was common and martyrdom came to be viewed as the highest calling possible for a Christian. In the fourth century, when Christianity became the official religion of the Roman empire, persecution stopped and martyrdom became rare. In order to continue to aspire to a higher calling, Christians replaced martyrdom with monasticism. Taking vows of celibacy and poverty was likened to the sacrifices of the martyrs.

Another factor was that "property was being left in rising amounts to individual churches; now and then a married priest had the bequest written in his name and transmitted it to his children."[21] To counteract such embezzlement, the church increasingly demanded that priests remain unmarried so as not to have any dependents who could benefit from the church's riches.

By the fourth century monasteries began to flourish and celibacy became the widespread ideal for clergy. By the fifth century various popes had issued decretals commanding certain degrees of clerical celibacy.[22] Soon the Catholic doctrine of clerical celibacy became official. At this point in church history the church had come to view celibacy as more spiritual and better than marriage.[23]

Even today the official position of the Catholic church is that the unmarried state is superior to marriage. Pope John Paul II writes,

In virginity or celibacy, the human being is awaiting, also in a bodily way, the eschatological marriage of Christ with the Church. . . . The celibate person thus anticipates in his or her flesh the new world of the future resurrection. . . . Virginity or celibacy, by liberating the human heart in a unique way, "so as to make it burn with greater love for God and all humanity," bears witness that the Kingdom of God and His justice is that pearl of great price which is preferred to every other value. . . . It is for this reason that the Church, throughout her history, has always defended the superiority of this charism to that of marriage by reason of the wholly singular link which it has with the Kingdom of God.[24]

The Reformation: The Protestant Pendulum Swing

Clerical celibacy was not without its problems. Right from the start, many who professed vows of celibacy overestimated their powers of self-control and fell into sexual sin.

Tertullian does not hesitate to assert that the desire of enjoying the reputation of virginity led to much secret immorality, the effects of which were concealed by infanticide. Cyprian chronicles, not with surprise but sorrow, the numerous instances which he had known of ruin resulting to those who had so fatally miscalculated their power of resistance. . . . and with a degree of common sense hardly to be looked for in so warm an admirer of the perfection of virginity, he advises that those whose weakness rendered doubtful the strict observance of their vows should return to the world and satisfy their longings in legitimate marriage.[25]

In the Great Schism of 1054, the Eastern Orthodox church split from Roman Catholicism over a number of doctrinal and ecclesiastical issues, including using unleavened bread in the Eucharist and adding the *filioque* clause to the Nicene Creed.[26] Interestingly enough, one of the reasons cited for the split was the enforcement of clerical celibacy because it was "contrary to apostolic example and ecclesiastical tradition."[27]

Unlike Roman Catholics, Orthodox priests were allowed to marry. Catholic priests clamored for the same privilege. "Just as the Greek and Russian Orthodox Church, after the schism of 1054, continued to permit marriage to its priests, so the clergy of the Roman Church demanded the same right; and since the canon law of their church refused this, they took concubines."[28]

By the sixteenth century, the doctrine of clerical celibacy had become little more than a sham, as priests and bishops illicitly maintained sexual relationships or secret marriages, often with nuns. Historian Will Durant records, "Some confessors solicited sexual favors from female penitents. Thousands of priests had concubines; in Germany nearly all. In Rome it was assumed that priests kept concubines, and some reports estimated the prostitutes there at 6,000 in a population not exceeding 100,000."[29] "It was a known fact that Renaissance popes had mistresses and children, and that the Swiss Bishop of Constance earned some 400 florins a year by fining his priests four florins for every child they fathered."[30] Such hypocrisy, and the doctrines that caused it, came under fire in the Reformation.

Protestant Reformers sought to renew a corrupt church. They called for a return to purity of doctrine and lifestyle, one based on the authority of Scripture and not the human traditions of the church, which had become corrupt over the centuries. By elevating the authority of the Bible, the Reformers threw out many things proclaimed to be unbiblical, including the veneration of relics, the doctrine of purgatory, indulgences, and prayers to Mary and the saints. The Reformers also threw out the Catholic doctrine of clerical celibacy.

As a monk, Martin Luther was no stranger to the vows of chastity. He concluded that celibacy was an unnecessary and unbiblical standard for service to God. While Luther believed that there were undoubtedly those who could stay unmarried for the purpose of ministry, he said, "But these are rare; not one in a thousand can do it: it is one of God's special miracles."[31]

Luther railed against the hypocrisy of sacerdotal concubinage, and he saw enforced celibacy as the cause of sexual immorality in the church. "If you are able to remain chaste and be pure by your own strength, why then do you vow to be chaste? Keep it, if you can; but it is a mere nothing that you should want to boast about your vow. . . . Do you want to know to whom you have vowed to keep chastity? I'll tell you: the miserable devil in hell and his mother."[32]

In Luther's time, little was said about the virtues of marriage. He blamed the Catholic church and the church fathers for "never having written anything good about marriage."[33] Because Luther believed that fewer than one in a thousand could possibly stay chaste, he concluded, "It is certainly a fact that he who refuses to marry must fall into immorality."[34] Therefore, he saw marriage as the cure for sexual immorality both inside and outside the church. He wrote, "Marriage may be likened to a hospital for incurables which prevents inmates from falling into a graver sin."[35] Echoing Old Testament and Greco-Roman norms, Luther said men should marry by age twenty and women between fifteen and eighteen.[36]

Luther rooted his arguments for marriage and family in the natural order. So strongly did he believe that marriage was the normative state that he said,

> A young woman, if the high and rare grace of virginity has not been bestowed upon her, can do without a man as little as without food, drink, sleep and other natural needs. And on the other hand: a man, too, cannot be without a woman. The reason is the following: begetting children is as deeply rooted in nature as eating and drinking. That is why God provided the body with limbs, arteries, ejaculation and everything that goes along with them. Now if someone wants to stop this and not permit what nature wants and must do, what is he doing but preventing nature from being nature, fire from burning, water from being wet, and man from either drinking, eating or sleeping?[37]

At age forty-two, Luther acted on his beliefs by marrying Catherine von Bora, a twenty-six-year-old runaway nun. This further symbolized his split with the Catholic church—a monk marrying a nun was scandalous. "Luther's wedding marked a radical break. . . . The Reformation had to take leave of the centuries-old ideal of the charismatic leader who, as an ascetic man of God, forsakes all things 'worldly.'"[38] Catholics condemned the marriage and expected that their "sacrilegious union" would spawn deformed children. The Luthers had six children, born healthy and free from birth defects, though two died in childhood.

The Swiss Reformer John Calvin also urged marriage over singleness. "For the majority of people, he taught, God not only permitted but positively *commanded* marriage; any who resisted matrimony fought against God. Only those who had been 'singled out by divine appointment' should remain unmarried."[39] At age thirty Calvin married a widow in order to escape the celibacy that he criticized as "a yoke imposed on priests shut up in a furnace of lust with perpetual fire."[40]

Thus we see the beginnings of the Reformation emphasis on marriage and family, once again alienating the single adult. Evangelical Protestants have followed this teaching ever since, as is evidenced in contemporary family movements such as the American Family Association, Focus on the Family and the Family Research Council. The modern-day emphasis on the "nuclear family" is largely a development of Western individualism and nineteenth-century industrial culture, rather than a following of biblical models of family, which tended to be multigenerational and included extended relatives.[41]

The Search for Balance

While both single and married persons played significant roles in the continuing work of Christianity, many singles have not been noted as singles. Besides Jesus and Paul, other New Testament singles include John the Baptist, Mary Magdalene, and Jesus' friends Mary, Martha and Lazarus. Paul's missionary colaborers who appear to have been single include Luke, Silas, Barnabas, Timothy, Titus, Epaphroditus, Apollos, Lydia, Dorcas and Phoebe. Acts 21:9 mentions that Philip's four prophetess daughters were all unmarried. In fact, not many married couples, such as Priscilla and Aquila, are specifically mentioned in the New Testament.

The early church leaders were almost entirely single, including saints and theologians such as Augustine, Francis of Assisi, Thomas Aquinas, Joan of Arc, Teresa of Avila, John of the Cross, Thomas à Kempis and Bernard of Clairvaux.

Even Protestant leaders who later married accomplished great things while they were single. When Martin Luther nailed his ninety-five theses to the Wittenberg church door, he was a thirty-three-year-old single adult. At the age of twenty-seven, single adult John Calvin published the first edition of his *Institutes of the Christian Religion*.

Francis Asbury, called "The Apostle of American Methodism," remained single his whole life. Asbury was a circuit-riding preacher throughout colonial America. When the Revolutionary War broke out, all British Methodist preachers returned to Great Britain except for Asbury, who stayed on and recruited new preachers for Methodism.[42]

During the nineteenth century, large numbers of single women committed their lives to overseas missionary work. The need for missionaries was so great that there were not enough married couples and male missionaries to meet the need. Women's missionary agencies were started in the 1860s and had great success throughout the next half-century. "In

1861 there was one single missionary in the field, Miss Marston, in Burma; in 1909, there were 4,710 unmarried women in the field."[43]

Twentieth-century examples of Christian singles include Dietrich Bonhoeffer, the German pastor and theologian who was executed in a Nazi concentration camp. C. S. Lewis was a bachelor for most of his life and remained a celibate widower after his brief marriage late in life. Anglican theologian and Bible expositor John Stott is another single church leader who has had a significant worldwide ministry.

The history of Christian singleness has been that of a pendulum swinging back and forth between two equally unhealthy extremes. Jewish society elevated marriage and family to the extent that it marginalized the single person. Religious leaders were always married. Then New Testament Christian teaching raised singleness to an equal level with marriage. Then the early church, influenced by Gnosticism, advocated an asceticism that taught singleness as the better way. Only worldly people married, while holy monks and nuns forsook marriage. In reaction to the abuses of enforced chastity, the Protestant Reformers rejected clerical celibacy and instead elevated marriage and family over singleness.

Historian Ruth Tucker comments about this historical shift: "We [Protestants] view the emphasis on celibacy in the Roman Catholic church as misdirected, and we can see the problems that have resulted from it. But it is entirely possible that we have gone to the other extreme, so that subconsciously we view singles as somehow defective."[44]

Just as the Catholic doctrine of clerical celibacy incorrectly overemphasizes celibacy as the Gnostics did, so also does Protestant "family theology" incorrectly overemphasize marriage and family as the Jews did.

Furthermore, Tucker says, family theology has gone too far.

The family has become such a high priority that young couples are questioning their call to missions because of family considerations. "Family has become a god in many churches, thereby throttling many potential missionaries," writes James Reapsome, editor of *Evangelical Missions Quarterly.* "Some churches are putting the married state, home comfort, and the education and happiness of children before world evangelization."

It is difficult to argue against the married state and the happiness of children, but these were not the number-one priorities of Jesus. "Family theology" is not biblical theology.[45]

A truly Christian view of both singleness and marriage will honor both equally without disparaging one or the other. Recovering such a balance is the first step toward a church where singles are valued equally with marrieds.

Discussion Questions

1. What do you find most significant in this historical survey? Do you think the pendulum-shift analogy is accurate?

2. Is your experience as a single more like living (a) in Jewish times, (b) in the early days of the church or (c) after the Reformation?

3. Does your church value singleness and marriage on an equal level, or is one more highly valued than the other?

3

·······················

THE MYTH OF THE GIFT

I wish that all were as I myself am. But each has a particular gift from God,
one having one kind and another a different kind.
1 CORINTHIANS 7:7 NRSV

"**D**o you have the gift of singleness?"

No question makes singles more uneasy. And no concept generates more confusion for singles. "Ah, the gift of singleness," one single friend mused. "Sometimes I wonder if it's like a Christmas gift you want to return. You know, you get something from someone, and you're like, 'Okay, this is nice, but I'd rather have another sweater than this one.' Well, I'd rather have the gift of marriage than this gift of singleness!"

"If you were to ask me, 'Do you think you have the gift of singleness?' I'd probably say no," Maria said. "If you asked me why, I guess because I have a desire to be a wife and mother, but I'm not necessarily sure that someone who has the gift of singleness doesn't have those desires—that they're completely not there. Some people imply that someone who has the gift of singleness doesn't even have a sex drive, and I'm not sure that's true."

Is there such a thing as "the gift of singleness" or "the gift of celibacy"? What is meant when people talk about a gift of singleness? And if it really is a gift, why doesn't anybody want it?

In this chapter we will examine the traditional view of the gift of singleness. We will see where these ideas come from, what problems this view may create, and how we've come to believe misconceptions about it. Then we will correct these misconceptions by examining the biblical material. Let's discover what Paul really meant when he talked about singleness as a gift.

The Traditional View of the Gift of Singleness

First, the Bible does not contain a formal definition of a "gift of singleness." Nowhere does any biblical writer clearly say anything like "The gift of singleness means that God makes you happy without marriage." The only reference to such a gift is found in Paul's words in 1 Corinthians 7:7: "I wish that all were as I myself am. But each has a particular gift from God, one having one kind and another a different kind" (NRSV).

Despite the lack of an explicit statement in Scripture, many Christians define the gift of singleness as some kind of supernatural empowerment that enables one to live as a single person without endless frustration at being unmarried. C. Peter Wagner defines the gift of celibacy as "the special ability that God gives to some members of the body of Christ to remain single and enjoy it; to be unmarried and not suffer undue sexual temptations." He says,

> If you are single and know down in your heart that you would get married in an instant if a reasonable opportunity presented itself, you probably don't have the gift of celibacy. If you are single and find yourself terribly frustrated by unfulfilled sexual impulses, you probably don't have the gift. But if neither of these things seems to bother you, rejoice—you may have found one of your spiritual gifts.[1]

Wagner's book provides a questionnaire to help readers identify their spiritual gifts. In this inventory, these five statements indicate a gift of singleness:

"I am single and enjoy it."

"Other people have noted that I feel more indifferent about not being married than most."

"I am glad I have more time to serve the Lord because I am single."

"I am single and have little difficulty controlling my sexual desires."

"I identify with Paul's desire for others to be single as he was."

According to Wagner, if you have these five characteristics, then you have the gift of singleness.

Another author defines the gift of singleness in this way: "The ability joyfully to embrace singleness as a lifetime commitment is a gift of God given to some but not others." This writer suggests that this ability to cope with singleness is an ability on a par with other talents, like music. "You either have a spiritual gift or you don't. The same point applies to the gift of singleness. It's a gift provided by God to some but not others. If God hasn't given it to me, there's no way I can attain it, any more than one without a gift of music can expect that practice will enable them to inspire others through their singing."[2]

According to this definition, the gift of singleness is something that God gives to help a single person handle the single life. Some singles have it and others don't. One commentator writes, "[Paul] is speaking about his own gift of continence. In respect to celibacy, he was given the grace to practice self-control. This does not mean that someone who is unable to do that and marries instead receives a special gift to engage in marriage. Paul prescribes no law or command. Each individual should decide this matter for himself."[3]

Some go further than this. One author writes, "He that has not received the gift of continence must marry, and must not try to remain unmarried. . . . He that does not possess it should marry."[4] In other words, singles who do not have the gift of singleness remain emotionally and sexually frustrated for good reason; God wants them to be married. The fact that they are not happily enjoying the single life is evidence of this. Or so the traditional view says.

A Problematic Myth

The traditional view of the gift of singleness raises more problems than it solves. The following are seven of those problems.

Problem #1: The traditional view judges the gift of singleness merely by a subjective feeling. According to the above authors, if I *feel* I wouldn't be happy as a lifelong single, then I probably don't have the gift. If I *desire* to marry and have children, I probably don't have the gift of singleness. It doesn't matter what my actual circumstances might be; all that matters is what I subjectively feel deep down in my heart.

The problem is this. Whether or not a single *feels* as if he or she has the gift of singleness, that single is still single! Regardless of any heartfelt desire for marriage, unless marriage takes place, that single person must still live as a single.

Many singles wonder if they have the gift of singleness, and most hope they don't. But think of how absurd this line of reasoning would be if we applied it to the state of marriage. Would a married person ever ask the question, "I wonder if I have the gift of marriage?" What if, after years of marriage, the partner has put on a few pounds, no longer seems attractive—the romance is gone? Maybe there are dirty diapers in the bathtub and arguments at every meal. What if this married person feels the pressures of marriage are just too much to handle? This person could then conclude, "Boy, this marriage business is getting tough. Well, I really don't *feel* like being married anymore. I guess I just must not have the gift of marriage." Would it then be permissible for such a person to leave the marriage?

Ridiculous as it sounds, this is exactly how many singles think about the gift of singleness. *If I don't feel I have the gift, or if I really don't want it, then I must not have it.* But a married person who doesn't feel very happy about the marriage should not question whether or not he or she has a particular gifting from God to be married. Rather, that person should do everything possible to improve the marriage, whether through communication skills, conflict resolution, changed priorities, counseling or marriage seminars. So too someone who is single, instead of wondering whether or not God has provided a particular gifting to be single—and instead of marrying the first person who comes along, just to be married—should take steps to live a healthy life as a single person.

And feelings change from year to year and even from day to day. A single may be comfortable being single one day but desire marriage the next. Does this indicate that the gift of singleness comes and goes? If such a gift were from God, one would expect it to be more consistent and less fickle.

Problem #2: This view of singleness minimizes the reality of temptation. Wagner's definition of the gift of celibacy says that those with the gift have the ability "to be unmarried and not suffer undue sexual temptations." What does he mean? One could take his statement in two ways: either God prevents the individual from encountering external temptations or he removes from the individual the internal desire to engage in sexual activity.

But is this true? Does God somehow miraculously remove all manner of sexual temptations from the single who has been gifted with the gift of celibacy? Do people who have the gift of celibacy really "have little difficulty controlling sexual desires"? Did Paul, who presumably had the gift of singleness, never face sexual temptation?

Paul nowhere says that he has any "peculiar gift of continence" or that he was "given the grace to practice self-control." To assume so is to read something into his words that isn't explicitly there. It is entirely possible that Paul may have struggled with temptation and even given in at times. In Romans 7, where he speaks at length about not doing what he ought and doing evil things he hates, Paul could have in mind sins of a sexual nature—actions or at least impure thoughts. It's speaking where the Bible is silent to presume that a supernatural gift of celibacy prevented Paul from ever falling into sexual sin.

Let us go one step further. If we take Scripture seriously, we understand that Jesus, an unmarried single man, is able to sympathize with our weaknesses because he was "tempted in every way, just as we are—yet was without sin" (Heb 4:15). Jesus shared full humanity with us, including all sexual and hormonal drives. Since he was a normal human being, he must have understood the potent power of sexual temptation.

Jesus had ample opportunity for sexual temptation. Some of his closest companions were "women of ill repute" who had been (or still were) prostitutes, adulterers and other "sinful women." Some commentators have suggested that the woman at the well in John 4 may have been there not just drawing water but cruising for sex. "This passage explodes with new meaning if this woman is 'hitting on' Jesus. To understand the difference, don't read this passage monotone; read it with a breathy 'I have no husband.' Add to it her seductive smile and half-opened eyes. It's not what she says to Jesus, it's what she's thinking. Her half-lie, 'I have no husband,' may be a way of saying, 'I'm available to you.'"[5]

It would be incorrect to say that Jesus never felt the tugs of sexual temptation. Rather, he was tempted in every way, just as we are, but he chose never to give in. This is not superhuman giftedness. This is simply living with holiness and integrity.

Problem #3: The traditional view creates an artificial two-tier class system of singles. If some singles have received a supernatural gift that enables them to live happy celibate lives, then by definition other singles have not. In other words, God has equipped *some* singles to live the single life effectively, but not *all* singles.

Such a construction is artificial and unbiblical. Scripture never gives justification for placing people into three groups: married, single with the gift and single without the gift. While he does distinguish between different kinds of singles, such as virgins and widows, Paul never talks to groups of singles based on their ability to live the single life. He does address certain groups: "Now to the unmarried and the widows I say . . ." (1 Cor 7:8); "To the married I give this command . . ." (1 Cor 7:10); "Now about virgins . . ." (1 Cor 7:25). But Paul never says things like "Now to singles who have the gift of singleness, I say this, and to singles who do not have the gift of singleness, I say this." Such a distinction is simply not there.

We may ask again: Would this two-tiered analogy hold true for the married life? Are there some married people who receive a supernatural gift to have good marriages and others who are not so equipped? I think not. Nobody would say that God gives some marriages the ability to do well and dooms others to failure. To do so is to deny responsibility for one's marriage and is tantamount to calling God the cause of divorce.

Some say that 1 Corinthians 7:9, "it is better to marry than to burn with passion," indicates two kinds of singles—those who should marry and those who shouldn't. However, Paul's comparison in this verse is between single life that lacks self-control and married life. Given the choice between sexual immorality and marriage, it is of course better that one's sexual activity be expressed within marriage. But Paul does not say that some singles have a supernatural gift that provides sexual self-control, nor does he say that singles without such a gift should marry.

Problem #4: While seeming to exalt singleness, the traditional view actually demeans singleness. On the one hand, the traditional view seems to make singleness a superspiritual calling available only to the truly holy. On the other hand, it subtly considers the single person abnormal for preferring the single life. Because it requires a special gift, singleness must be horrible, a painful thing to be endured. The gift of singleness, then, is like anesthesia during surgery or Novocain for a tooth drilling. Between the lines is the idea that nobody would ever make a conscious choice to stay single if he or she had the opportunity to marry. Therefore, they must have some special gifting that makes them refuse the married state. Marriage is seen as normative, and for somebody not to want to be married is unusual at best and bizarre at worst.

This perception is unbiblical. "Paul gives no hint that marriage is normal while celibacy is a 'special' condition only for those who are called to it. It is, like marriage, open to all."[6]

We must ask ourselves, Would either Jesus or Paul teach something that relegated some followers to a second-class status? If we believe in a doctrine that elevates one form of living over another, then something is wrong. Neither Jesus nor Paul endorsed any such distinctions. They did not say, for instance, that being a Jewish Christian was better than being a Gentile Christian or vice versa. Both are equally good ways to serve God. So too with the states of singleness and marriage. A view that demeans one and elevates the other is inaccurate and unchristian.

Problem #5: The idea of a gift of supernatural empowerment for singleness is unbiblical. Scripture nowhere says that the gift of singleness bestows some supernatural empowerment to live singly with no desire for marriage. Some interpreters read Matthew 19:12, "Some have made themselves eunuchs for the kingdom of heaven," as evidence that those with the gift of singleness no longer have any sex drive whatsoever, presuming that Christian celibates will resemble secular eunuchs in the area of sexuality. But is Jesus' point here that Christian "eunuchs for the kingdom of heaven" share the same sexuality traits as other eunuchs? No, Jesus is not implying that Christian celibates must be physically castrated in order to truly be eunuchs for the kingdom. Jesus' point is not that eunuchs lack sexual desire, but rather that eunuchs are uniquely positioned to serve their king singlemindedly, as we saw in chapter two. The primary point of the comparison is the service and devotion of the eunuchs to their lord, not their sex life (or lack thereof).

Paul's teaching similarly lacks support for the supernatural view of the gift of singleness. In 1 Corinthians 7 we do not find any mystical language whatsoever that suggests that God will somehow magically transform the single person's disposition and remove all marital longings.

On the contrary, the chapter is extremely matter-of-fact. Paul observes that those who marry will face many troubles (v. 28) and that singles are able to be concerned about serving God without worrying about serving their families as marrieds must do (vv. 32-34). A married person's interests, by definition, are divided between family and everything else. This is no divinely revealed insight; there is nothing superspiritual about it. This is merely common sense. Paul even says that there is no command from the Lord on this; he gives his opinion "as one who by the Lord's mercy is trustworthy" (v. 25).

Therefore, it goes against the grain of the whole chapter to read verse 7 as being an indication of any supernatural gifting to be single. Furthermore, it seems odd to define this gift of singleness as the ability to "joyfully embrace" lifelong singleness (as Wagner says) when there is no such comparable statement for the gift of marriage. Married people are repeatedly exhorted to love one another and honor their marriage commitment, but nowhere are they assured that they will receive a divine gift that enables them continually to "joyfully embrace" marriage as a lifetime commitment. Unfortunately, the fact that Christians are as prone to divorce as the general population seems to indicate that such a gift does not exist—at least not in some automatic, supernatural way that keeps marriages glued together. If such a gift is not available for married people, should we expect a similar gift for singles?

Problem #6: The traditional view confuses the gift of singleness with a healthy self-identity. One single said, "When I've taken spiritual gift inventories, I've ranked high on having the gift of singleness. But I don't know if their understanding of singleness is the right understanding, because I'm comfortable with who I am before God, and I'd be comfortable being married too."

The traditional view presupposes that desire for marriage is normative and that to be satisfied as a single person is abnormal. But this penalizes the virtue of contentment. Christians are called to find contentment whatever their status in life. A Christian who learns to be content with areas such as socioeconomic status and physical appearance will also be content with his or her marital status, whether married or single. This is not evidence of a gift of singleness. This is Christian maturity.

Problem #7: The traditional view is spiritually abusive. It is pastorally insensitive to counsel that singles who do not feel they have a supernatural gift of continence "must marry." The fact of the matter is that someone who earnestly believes that he or she does not have the gift of singleness may still never marry. We may sincerely desire with our entire soul to be married. But circumstances may dictate that we never find someone suitable for a marriage partner. And the result can be doubt and resentment.

Singles who have this flawed theology of singleness end up blaming God. Such a single may feel cheated. He or she may cry out to God, "I truly believe and feel deep down in my heart that I am meant to be married! If I don't have the gift of celibacy, I'm supposed to get married, right? Then why haven't you given me a partner?" Feeling like victims who were given a gift they did not want, many singles become angry, resentful and bitter because they believe this teaching.

So something is wrong with the traditional view of the gift of singleness. It does not make adequate sense of the biblical material. Is there another way to think about this gift? We need to reexamine what Paul actually said and develop a new understanding of what is meant by the gift of singleness.

"Gift" Versus "Spiritual Gift"

Where do we get the idea that the gift of singleness is a God-given, divine ability to be happy with being single? It comes primarily from a confusion in our concept of spiritual gifts. The only place in Scripture where the word "gift" (Greek *charisma*) is used in conjunction with marital status is found in 1 Corinthians 7:7, where Paul says, "Each has a particular gift from God, one having one kind and another a different kind" (NRSV).

Paul never uses the phrase "gift of singleness" or "gift of celibacy." This is not part of his terminology or vocabulary. The phrase itself is unbiblical. Paul does refer to the "unmarried" (Greek *agamos*) in 1 Corinthians 7:8, 32, 34. (Verse 27, "Are you unmarried?" [NIV] is literally, "Are you free from a wife?") But Paul never connects this word for "unmarried" in the same phrase with the word for "gift." By Paul's language, there is no such thing as a *charisma agamou*, a gift of unmarriedness or singleness.

1 Corinthians 12

The confusion in the traditional view comes from misinterpreting and combining two passages. In order to understand where contemporary views of the gift of singleness come from, we must turn several chapters forward in the book of 1 Corinthians to chapter 12. There Paul says, "Now concerning spiritual gifts [literally, "about spiritual things"], brothers and sisters, I do not want you to be uninformed" (1 Cor 12:1 NRSV). He goes on to say that "there are varieties of gifts, but the same Spirit . . . and there are varieties of activities, but it is the same God who activates all of them in everyone" (vv. 4-6 NRSV).

From this chapter we see that God, through the Holy Spirit, empowers his people with certain gifts of ministry. That is why they're called *spiritual* gifts; the Holy *Spirit* is actively at work in each gift to accomplish a particular task or function, in the context of the ministry of the church. "Now to each one the manifestation of the Spirit is given for the common good" (v. 7). So there is an agent of action—the Spirit. And there is a purpose—the common good of Christians in the fellowship of the body. Whether wisdom or knowledge or faith or healing or prophecy, "all these are the work of one and the same Spirit" (v. 11). This is the purpose of a spiritual gift.

Here is a crucial distinction. Throughout chapter 12, Paul declares that all these gifts are *spiritual* gifts, that is, Spirit-empowered for a particular function. In verses 8 and 9, "one person is given *through the Spirit* the message of wisdom; to another the message of knowledge comes *by means of the same Spirit*; to another faith *by the same Spirit,* to another gifts of healing *by that one Spirit,*" and so on. Paul clearly emphasizes that the Spirit personally empowers each of these gifts. The Holy Spirit is at work in an individual to accomplish some particular work for the common good of the church.

1 Corinthians 7

However, this kind of language is entirely absent in 1 Corinthians 7. There, Paul says only that some have one gift and others have another. Nowhere is the Holy Spirit mentioned for the empowerment of that gift. Nowhere is the gift called a "spiritual gift," only a gift.

That makes all the difference. It is a mistake to consider singleness (or marriage) as being the same kind of gift as the spiritual gifts listed in chapter 12. The words and the context are different. The traditional view assumes that because all of the functional gifts in chapter 12 are Spirit-empowered, then the gift of singleness must also be a special, divine, spiritual empowerment. This is simply not true. That word is just not there. The idea of "gift as supernatural empowerment" comes from our own romanticized ideal for singleness, as we have seen in church history, and not from the actual biblical text.

The New Testament uses "gift" in several instances where it does not indicate any supernatural empowerment. For example, eternal life is a gift, as it says in Romans 6:23: "The gift of God is eternal life." In this case, the gift is not some function for ministry; rather, it is an objective gift. You simply receive and accept the gift of eternal life. Singleness and marriage, if they are to be considered gifts, are more like the gift of eternal life than like the spiritual gifts of 1 Corinthians 12. One either has eternal life or doesn't. One either is married or is single.

The gifts in 1 Corinthians 12 are *functional* gifts, descriptive of specific tasks within a ministry situation. That is why they are "spiritual"; the Holy Spirit empowers each one in the context of ministry. Someone with the gift of teaching has the function of teaching others and is Holy Spirit-empowered to use that gift to teach. One who has the gift of serving has the function of serving others and does so through the work of the Spirit.

This is not the case with singleness. Singleness is not a functional gift; there is no such action as "singling." Being single or married does not in itself enable you to preach a sermon or teach a Sunday-school class—or prevent you from doing so. Paul talks about two different kinds of gifts. While one might legitimately call singleness a gift, it is incorrect to call it a *spiritual* gift.

Singleness and Marriage As Equal Gifts

This is the implication: The "gift of singleness" is not something that must be spiritually discerned or subjectively felt. Singles do not need to search their hearts to see if they are truly able to live as contented singles. It is not some supernatural empowerment for some function of ministry. Rather, the gift is a description of an objective status. *If you are single, then you have the gift of singleness. If you are married, you don't.* If you marry, you exchange the gift of singleness for the gift of marriedness. Both are good. Simple as that.

Read verse 7 again in this light. "I wish that all were as I myself am [single]. But each has a particular gift from God, one having one kind [singleness] and another a different kind [marriage]" (NRSV). This is the essence of the verse. It does not make sense to take this verse as meaning that some singles have the gift of singleness and some singles have a gift of nonsingleness. The fact that each one has a particular gift from God implies that these two gifts are mutually exclusive. If you have one, you don't have the other. While this is not true of the functional spiritual gifts—one person may have several at once—it is certainly true of singleness and marriage. Everybody is either one or the other.

Eugene Peterson's paraphrase *The Message* is helpful here, as it renders this passage in a way so Paul's meaning is very clear: "Sometimes I wish everyone were single like me—a simpler life in many ways! But celibacy is not for everyone any more than marriage is. God gives the gift of the single life to some, the gift of the married life to others."

To read the passage in this way removes any ambiguity when it comes to what Paul means by the gift. The two gifts of 1 Corinthians 7:7 are simply singleness and marriage. Neither is a supernatural empowerment, and the gift is not some special grace to live as a single or as a married person. Paul is telling singles and marrieds alike to acknowledge that both statuses are gifts of God, to be honored and treasured.

Historically, many commentators have construed Paul's advice here as a statement of the inherent superiority of celibacy. They presume that "the truly 'spiritual' are celibate; for the rest there is the 'concession' to marriage, which exists basically to curb illicit desire. But Paul would have none of this. For him both marriage and celibacy are gifts, and despite his own preference for his gift, he certainly does not raise it to a higher spirituality. That is to fly full in the face of the text itself."[7]

Furthermore, the gift of singleness, understood in this sense, does not determine an unalterable lifelong future for anyone. In fact, *everybody* starts out with the gift of singleness. Mennonite theologian John Howard Yoder writes, "It needs to be taught as normative Christian truth that singleness is the first normal state for every Christian."[8] "There is nothing special about being single," one single woman wrote. "Everybody is single at least once and often single again. Only the duration and quality of singleness differ."[9] The "gift" of singleness is *descriptive*, not *restrictive*. It does not prevent you from getting married if you so desire and circumstances permit.

Verses 36-38 in this chapter make it clear that Paul thinks it's equally acceptable for a person to get married or to stay single. He writes in response to those who think that singleness is somehow a better state and it may be sinful to marry. Peterson's *The Message* reads:

If a man has a woman friend to whom he is loyal but never intended to marry, having decided to serve God as a "single," and then changes his mind, deciding he should marry her, he should go ahead and marry. It's no sin; it's not even a "step down" from celibacy, as some say. On the other hand, if a man is comfortable in his decision for a single life in service to God and it's entirely his own conviction and not imposed on him by others, he ought to stick with it. Marriage is spiritually and morally right and not inferior to singleness in any way, although as I indicated earlier, because of the times we live in, I do have pastoral reasons for encouraging singleness.

Simon Kistemaker says of this passage, "Is [Paul] advocating celibacy rather than marriage? Not at all. Paul teaches that although marriage, which God instituted, is good and commendable, not every person should be married or seek marriage."[10]

So what are we to say about singles who don't like being single? Many try to deny the gift of singleness. They say that they don't want it, because they assume gifts are permanent and they don't want to be single all their lives. In that case, they can get married. Of course, this depends on finding a suitable and willing partner. But nothing inherent to singleness will prevent someone from leaving the single state to be married. People do it every day. God does not supernaturally intervene to stop the wedding ceremony of two people who, up until that point, are single and have the gift of singleness. When they say "I do," then they receive the gift of marriage.

It is rude to *refuse* a gift and throw it back in the giver's face. However, it can be entirely appropriate to *exchange* a gift for a different one of equal value. Think about taking a Christmas gift back to the store. You can't exchange it for something that's more expensive. But you can exchange it for something of the *same* value.

So it is with marriage and singleness. When a single gets married, it is not a rejection of the gift of singleness. Nor is marriage a promotion, a step up to a more valued position, a more expensive Christmas gift. Rather, it is exchanging one gift for another one of equal value. One is not necessarily better than the other; both have their own advantages and disadvantages.

No Two-Tier System

This "egalitarian" view of singleness and marriage is tremendously liberating. A single who understands singleness in this way no longer has to be tortured with convoluted questioning as to whether or not he or she has the gift of singleness. Now all singles can know where they stand. All singles are on even ground. No two-tier system of singleness exists. All singles are free either to be single or to marry if they so desire and have opportunity. They needn't wonder why God hasn't supernaturally deadened all desire for marital companionship.

It also legitimizes the desire for a spouse. A single is free to date actively, to develop a relationship that can result in marriage. A single is equally free to abstain from the whole dating scene if he or she so chooses.

Consequently, we can affirm this principle: *The challenge is to make a success of the single life if you are single and make a success of the married life if you are married.* Whichever one you happen to be, do your best to be a good steward of that gift. If you are single, then you can develop a healthy Christian single life. And if the opportunity should come for you to exchange the gift of singleness for the gift of marriage, then feel free do so. But your ultimate priority is not whether or not you will marry; in either state, your ultimate concern is serving God.

This makes sense in the context of Paul's message to both singles and marrieds in 1 Corinthians 7:17: "Don't be wishing you were someplace else or with someone else. Where you are right now is God's place for you. Live and obey and love and believe right there. God, not your marital status, defines your life" *(The Message).*

In his meditation on Jesus' words "Consider the lilies of the field . . ." (Mt 6:28), Oswald Chambers says, "They grow where they are planted. Many of us refuse to grow where God plants us. Therefore, we don't take root anywhere."[11]

Rodney Clapp simply states: "Are you single? Then live as a Christian in that state. Are you married? Then live as a Christian in that state."[12]

Contentment in either state is important because either one may be temporary. One marriage partner or the other will eventually become single again, whether by death or divorce. You may lose a spouse to an accident or disease. It is rare for both partners to die simultaneously. Walter Trobisch has written, "Whether we are married or single, let us not make the mistake of thinking that our present state is permanent. . . . Marriage can be a task for a limited time and then it suddenly ends with the death of one partner. Being single can also be but a passing task."[13]

Because marriage and singleness are equal gifts, both states have their own joys and their own problems. At times, the other state seems more attractive. "Marriage has been likened to the situation of flies at the window: those on the inside want out, and those on the outside want in. Singles think the chief end of man is to get married, while many marrieds secretly long to be single again."[14] The grass is always greener.

So singles and marrieds may perceive each other at times. But as psychologist Paul Tournier has written, "The real problem is to make a success of one's marriage if one does marry, and to make a success of the celibate life if one does not. Each vocation is as difficult as the other."[15]

Both singleness and marriage are gifts to be honored and treasured. "The task we have to face is the same, whether we are married or single: To live a fulfilled life in spite of many unfulfilled desires."[16]

The booklet *Discovering Your Spiritual Gifts* by J. E. O'Day is one of the few works I have seen that includes both singleness and marriage in a list of gifts.[17] On the other hand, Wagner's inventory lists celibacy as a gift but does not include marriage. This is incorrect. Either they are both gifts on an equal level, as Paul says in 1 Corinthians 7:7, or neither one is a gift, since neither one is a functional gift. Both singleness and marriage are "manifestations of the grace of God, to be undertaken and to be sustained purely in the strength which the Lord daily supplies. . . . There is no less need of a gift of grace to use marriage Christianly than to live Christianly in celibacy."[18]

"Marriage and singleness constitute two equal and reciprocal options for expressing our identity as sexual beings," theologian Stanley Grenz writes. "It means that neither is to be elevated above the other, nor is either life choice to be deprecated as being of inferior worth."[19]

May the church come to recognize the equality of singleness and marriage—and to value all single and married people as being of equal worth to God. And as single Christians, may we value our own lives and situations in the way God does.

Discussion Questions

1. What have you heard in churches about the "gift of singleness"?
2. How have you experienced distortions or misconceptions of the gift of singleness?
3. "If you are single, you have the gift of singleness. If you are married, you don't." Does this teaching make sense to you? Why or why not?
4. "The challenge is to make a success of the single life if you are single and make a success of the married life if you are married." What are some steps you can take?

4

THE ISSUE OF GOD'S WILL

If marriage is good, singleness is also good. . . .
Neither is in itself better or worse than the other.
JOHN STOTT

My last name, Hsu, is pronounced "she," as in "She went to the store." Ever since high school, my friends have joked that I should marry a girl named Sue, so her name could be Sue Hsu—which would be pronounced "sushi." Though that might be cruel and unusual punishment, every time I've met somebody named Sue, Susie or Susan, I have always wondered, "Could this be the one?"

My junior year of college, I met a young woman my age from a different college at an intercollegiate Christian retreat. She had a prominent role as a student leader, and I noticed her because of her engaging, bubbly personality. The fact that she was a cute strawberry blond didn't hurt, either. I introduced myself to her, and she said, "My name is Susan." My internal radar went ballistic.

After getting to know her somewhat at several retreats, I wrote her a letter. To my surprise she responded immediately. So I wrote back, and we exchanged seven letters in seven weeks. We discovered that we had an incredible number of common interests and experiences. I had gone on choir tours to Canada and Colorado during college. She had gone on choir tours to Canada and Colorado during high school. She was on a Christian music outreach team that sang in churches. So was I. Both of us had taken two years of Greek as part of our studies. I had one younger brother; she had one younger sister. We were both from the western suburbs of Minneapolis; in fact, our hometowns were only twenty minutes apart.

We were both home for Easter weekend, and we got together three times in three days. We went to each other's churches, saw *Aladdin* together (I think it was the third time for both of us), and spent time together at the piano, with her singing as I played. Our friendship was growing, and I sensed a real possibility of developing a romantic relationship.

Then she invited me to visit her at her college. I went, hoping that we would initiate an official dating relationship. I wasn't disappointed. The weekend was like something straight out of a romantic movie. We went out for coffee, took a late-night stroll along a river and talked of our dreams and hopes in life. We discovered that we both liked mushroom-and-Swiss burgers. Even silly little things matched, like the fact that I still had a retainer cemented in behind my lower teeth and so did she. Every new fact seemed to be one more confirmation, "She's the one! She's the one!"

And so we professed our "like" for each other and began what could be called a whirlwind romance. We skipped through parks and playgrounds together. We went to church together Sunday morning, which happened to be Mother's Day, and the sermon was about "finding someone suitable" for healthy marital relationships. It was a sign from God. I was sure of it.

I was so ecstatic at the end of the weekend that I got a speeding ticket driving home. I didn't care. When I got home, I left my keys in the door lock all night. The next day I went to the mall and locked my keys in the car. I was floating on cloud nine, and my brain was somewhere on outer Neptune.

But it didn't last. The very next week Susan called and said that our weekend together had been wonderful, but it seemed unreal. We had pursued each other, and we had caught each other, but now what? She was having doubts—uncertainties about herself and our relationship. Sadly, there was to be no "happily ever after" for us. We broke up within a month.

I was devastated. What went wrong? Everything had been so perfect; I had been so sure that she was God's will for me. I had found the woman of my dreams—my Susan!—and then she was gone.

Can We Know God's Will?

Singleness and marriage are equal gifts before God, and it is a myth to believe that singleness is some divine gift for living the single life with ease. But another question may yet arise. Does God still call some people to the single life? Does God's will determine that some people will remain single and others not? And if so, how can we know?

Sometimes we feel at a loss as to what God's will is, and we ask for guidance. Other times we feel absolutely certain about his will—and discover we are completely wrong. And so we wonder, "Does God have a plan for our lives? And if he does, can we know what it is?"

Commentators are divided on whether or not God has a specific individual will for each person.[1] Some say that there is an overall general will but God does not have an actual preference for our individual decisions—whether we wear a red shirt or a blue one, or whether we marry one person or another. On the other hand, some say that God does have an individual will for us, but we must exercise our own free will and choose to follow God's guidance as we make decisions.

This book is not the place for an extended discussion of these issues, since there are many good books on the topic of God's guidance. I will limit this chapter to the question of discerning God's will as it relates to singleness, but first a few general comments.

Some have said that 95 percent of God's will for us has already been revealed to us in Scripture—things such as the qualitative characteristics of a godly, Christian life. For example, Paul says, "Be joyful always; pray continually; give thanks in all circumstances, for this is God's will for you in Christ Jesus" (1 Thess 5:16-18). Likewise, he writes, "It is God's will that you should be sanctified: that you should avoid sexual immorality; that each of you should learn to control his own body in a way that is holy and honorable, not in passionate lust . . . and that . . . no one should wrong his brother or take advantage of him" (1 Thess 4:3-6). In this sense, God's will is his desire for everybody to live by moral principles of Christian living.

M. Blaine Smith makes a very helpful distinction in terminology in defining God's will. God's will does not mean that we have no choice in the matter. Rather, God's will is simply what he desires for our lives, whether we choose it or not. He writes,

Whenever the New Testament refers to our responsibility for knowing or doing God's will, the Greek term used for *will* is always *thelema*, which generally implies not God's resolute intention but simply his wish or desire, which requires our cooperation for its fulfillment.

When Paul states, for instance, "this is the will of God, your sanctification: that you abstain from unchastity" (1 Thess 4:3), he's not talking about something God plans to do regardless of our cooperation. Rather, he's stating a *wish* God has for our behavior—one which we can choose to obey or not.[2]

Some believe that God both knows and ordains the events of our lives. Others think that God knows but does not ordain. Yet others say that God limits his own knowledge of the future. Whatever the extent of God's foreknowledge of our lives, most Christians would agree that we are not robots. In order to truly love and follow God, we must have the ability to *choose* to do so. Otherwise we are no more than puppets on a string, and our love and service to God are coerced and not authentic. Therefore, we have the ability to make responsible decisions.

So how do we make decisions that are in line with God's will? Some advocate a "five-finger" process of discerning God's will in decision-making, corresponding with the five fingers of the hand for easy memorization. The five elements are as follows.

1. God's general will. The crucial "thumb" for all decision-making, Scripture provides essential principles of moral and ethical behavior for all Christians.

2. Prayer. Bill Hybels writes, "Most of the time we think of prayer as talking to God, rarely stopping to wonder whether God might want to talk to us."[3] God may give us insights or leadings that will provide discernment through prayer.

3. Godly counsel. Trusted Christians can help us see the wisdom of our choices.

4. Circumstances. Opportunities can present us with paths that we should follow. Or doors can slam shut.

5. Inner peace. Though the least significant of these five criteria, we may have an intuitive sense of what to do.[4]

Furthermore, throughout the discernment process we must exercise proper use of the mind and reason. In his classic work *Knowing God*, J. I. Packer writes, "The fundamental mode whereby our rational Creator guides his rational creatures is by rational understanding and application of his written Word."[5] We should not expect that God will provide unique, supernatural revelation when he has already made most of his will known through Scripture.

John Stott provides this illustration on how one is to make decisions. He writes that Scripture has much to say on the subject of marriage. However:

But Scripture will not tell you whether your wife is to be Jane or June or Joan or Janet! How then are you to decide this major question? There is only one possible answer, namely by using the mind and the common sense which God has given you. Certainly you will pray for God's guidance. And if you are wise, you will ask the advice of your parents and of other mature people who know you well. But ultimately you must make up your mind, trusting that God will guide you through your own mental processes.[6]

With these general principles in mind, let us now examine three common misconceptions about God's will as it relates to singleness.

The Myth of the Marital Mandate

1. *"God wants all people to be married."* Some Christians believe that marriage is God's intent for everybody and that only people who were outside his will would remain unmarried. As support, they cite Genesis 2:18, where God says, "It is not good that the man should be alone. I will make a helper suitable for him." God then created Eve to be Adam's wife and partner. From this passage, many conclude that since God declared "good" everything he created except being alone, therefore God's design is for all to marry. Some theologians further suggest that because God created people in his image both male and female, an individual is an incomplete representation of the image of God until he or she finds a spouse. Then, as man and woman united in one flesh, the two together represent the image of God in its fullness.

In response to this point of view, we must recognize what the Genesis passage does and does not say. Because it is a narrative passage, we must be careful about reading general instructions for all people when we really only have a description of what God did in the case of Adam and Eve. Clearly the first man needed a woman if the human race was to have any offspring. As far as we know, God did not design Adam to reproduce the way that amoebas do. A safe conclusion one may make from reading this passage is that "if you ever discover that you are the only surviving representative of your sex in the world, and you come across your only existing counterpart, the two of you should consider marriage."[7]

The passage does affirm that human beings need companionship. God said that it is not good for the man to be alone. However, he did *not* say that it is not good for the man to be *unmarried*. Aloneness is what is not good here, not the lack of a spouse. God created people as social beings, built for relationship. It is entirely possible to live a complete life as a single person, as long as one lives in the context of a community of good friendships and relationships.

Jesus was our ultimate example of this. Who would ever go up to Jesus and quote Genesis 2:18 at him? Would anybody dare to tell him, "Y'know, Jesus, God said that it's not good for a man to be alone. I think it's about time you found a nice girl and settled down"? Tim Stafford writes, "Imagine, if you can, patronizing Jesus as a single person. 'Why haven't you ever married?' he is asked. 'You seem like such a nice person. I have a cousin in Bethsaida I'd really like you to meet. . . .'"[8]

On the contrary, if someone had objected to Jesus' singleness and said that it was not good for him to be alone, he very well might have motioned to his disciples and other followers and said, "But look around me. I'm not alone. I have these twelve who go with me everywhere. They have seen me through everything I have experienced in the last three years. I have other close friends, such as Mary, Martha and Lazarus. Remember, I said that whoever does the will of my Father is my mother and brother and sister. My followers are my family, and they are as close to me as a bride to a bridegroom."

Similarly, Paul is an example of one who was single but not alone. Paul never traveled by himself on his missionary travels. He took Barnabas and John Mark with him on his first missionary journey. On his second trip he was accompanied by Silas, and he picked up Timothy and Luke along the way. Acts 20:4 says that besides Timothy and Luke, Paul was joined by Sopater, Aristarchus, Secundus, Gaius, Tychicus and Trophimus. They spent time with and often stayed with the men and women of the church in each city. In some situations, such as his escape to Athens from Berea, persecution forced Paul to travel alone, but even then he left instructions for Silas and Timothy to join him as soon as possible (Acts 17:15). Clearly Paul's preference was to travel and minister with others.

God designed human beings to live in relationship with one another, but this does not mean that God's will for all is marriage. We will look at this subject further in chapter 7.

The Fallacy of Finding the Perfect Partner

2. *"God has someone picked out for me. I just have to find that person."* When the movie *The Bridges of Madison County* came out, Jenny insisted that Lora just had to go see it. Lora did. While she thought the cinematography was okay, she didn't like the movie as a whole because it endorsed adultery.

"But don't you see?" Jenny told her. "He was her *soulmate.*" While Meryl Streep's character loved her husband, their relationship did not have the total emotional and spiritual bond that characterized her affair with Clint Eastwood's character. That was because her husband was not her true "soulmate," Jenny claimed, while the visiting photographer was. So in her view the movie was tragic because these two people (who were supposed to be together) weren't able to live happily ever after.

"I think the reason Jenny identified with this movie so much is because she's not happy with her own marriage," Lora said. "I think she thinks that she married the wrong person and her 'soulmate' is still out there somewhere."

Christians rightly object to how such a worldview is used to justify adultery. But we still wonder: Does each of us have a "soulmate" or "missisng half" that we are supposed to find? Does God have one person picked out for us with whom we can have the perfect relationship? And if we marry the wrong person, are we doomed to never experience the ideal, blissful relationship that God intended for us?

Christians sometimes use the phrase, "That's a marriage that was made in heaven." I once saw a wall hanging that said, "Are marriages made in heaven? Maybe, but so are tornadoes."

Family counselor J. Allan Petersen, who writes on the topic of Christian infidelity, contends that one of the main causes of marital breakup is belief in the myth of marriages "made in heaven." He describes the assumptions behind this idea:

> The unspoken suppositions of this myth go like this: "Since heaven is a perfect place, any plan coming out of there brings with it its own suc-

cess. There is only one right man or one right woman—the one person in the world I can be happy with—with whom I am really compatible. And God has settled it that we will get together somehow. And further-more, if God chooses my partner for me and brings us together, we will surely not have the problems and difficulties other couples have. Little or no adjustment will be necessary. We are made for each other."[9]

Such a belief is expressed in popular love songs that say lovers are born or made for each other and in wedding songs that declare that God has brought the happy couple together.

God As Matchmaker

This view of God leads many on a frustrating quest. Singles pastor Rick Stedman writes,

The notion that God has already chosen a certain, specific person to be one's mate diminishes the role of personal choice and free will. Instead, it fosters the idea that each person must try to find God's perfect will in its absolute and inflexible specificity. Such singles end up as frustrated as the proverbial farm boy who had to search for a needle in a haystack.[10]

The result is that out of the 5.8 billion people on the planet, Christians try to find the one unique individual whom they believe God has picked for them.

This view leads to unrealistic expectations. If you believe that God has somebody out there for you, then that person must be perfect. After all, it's God's pick, right? This belief in God's ideal choice, Smith says, "leads some to be too idealistic about whom they will consider marrying. Since God is perfect, it is felt that you must not settle for anyone who less than fully measures up to your image of the ideal mate. Such persons are quick to bail out of a relationship at the first sign of another's imperfections, while others wait endlessly for that perfect relationship that never comes along."[11]

While many Christian singles believe in the dream of the perfect part-ner, most don't realize that this concept comes not from the Bible, but from Greek philosophy. The belief that "there is only one person in the world for me, without whom I am lost" was first articulated by Plato. Diane Ackerman writes, "This romantic ideal of the perfect partner was invented by Plato. It appealed so strongly to hearts and minds that people believed it in all the following centuries, and many still believe it today."[12]

The myth of the perfect partner stems from Plato's view that everything in the material world is merely a temporary copy of an ideal, universal and perfect form. The implication for relationships, Plato suggests, is that we have an innate, preconceived image of the one person we are meant to be with, and our unending quest is for a human facsimile who will match that perfect ideal.

Furthermore, Ackerman writes, "to Plato, lovers are incomplete halves of a single puzzle, searching for each other in order to become whole." In *The Symposium,* Plato articulates the view that originally there were three sexes: men, women, and a combination of man and woman that had two heads, two pairs of arms, two sets of genitals and so on. However, Zeus was threatened by the potential power of these hermaphrodites, so he divided each one in half. Therefore, since each person longs for the missing half, we spend our lives searching for that missing part of us in order to be reunited and become one again.[13]

So runs the myth that each one of us is an incomplete half searching for the perfect other half who will make us whole. This belief runs completely counter to biblical teaching. We are not the divided remnants of a third gender. Scripture affirms that each of us is a whole person by ourself, because we are created in the image of God as whole beings and our sense of wholeness and identity comes from our identity in Christ. We are not halves looking for another half or a melody looking for a harmony. Christians, created as whole persons and redeemed out of our fallenness to be whole persons, must not replace the truths of Scripture with the misguided claims of Greek philosophy.

The view of God as matchmaker also makes us passive and reactive. According to this view, "faith demands that you sit still and wait for God to bring the right person to your doorstep. . . . Some are left thinking that the burden is completely upon God to bring results. They think that we have no responsibility for the outcome."[14]

By that argument, high school students should never apply for college. God has a college picked out for each one, so there's no point in applying to colleges that aren't the right one. A student should just sit at home and wait for the acceptance letter to arrive. The same thing could be said about finding a job. One could think, "If God has a specific job out there for me, the employer will just give me a call and hire me. I don't have to do anything." As irresponsible and unrealistic as this approach may be, this is exactly how many Christians expect God to drop the perfect mate into their lap, without any initiative or responsibility on their part.

Furthermore, viewing God as matchmaker causes the blame for any problems to be placed on God. "If God predestined us for this relationship and it doesn't work out, it's his fault. . . . [We say] 'I guess God didn't really bring us together in the first place. Maybe our marriage was only secular and God wasn't really in it. He really didn't bind us together, so we'd better separate.'"[15]

> The idea that God has a perfect mate chosen for each person becomes twisted when the marriage goes sour. God then becomes the responsible party for choosing the mate, and the blame for the failed relationship is loaded upon God rather than on the individuals involved. If divorce follows, God may become the scapegoat.[16]

Another error, opposite of viewing God as divine matchmaker, is to think that God has nothing to do with the decision at all. People with this view go out and do everything in their own human power to find the right mate. They have no regard for God's guidance or counsel.

God As Partner

Contrary to either extreme, God's will for our lives is much more of a cooperative effort, a partnership between God and us acting together. Blaine Smith says, "The Bible in general views the responsibility as a cooperative one, where both God and we play a part in the process."[17] Similarly, Petersen points out that even God putting Adam and Eve together did not guarantee family success. He counsels couples, "I do not know whether or not your marriage was made in heaven, but I do know that all the maintenance work is done on earth."[18]

Smith points out, "Scripture never specifically states that God predestines a man and woman for each other in marriage."[19] The language of 1 Corinthians 7 argues against the myth of the divine matchmaker. When Paul advises widows who are wondering what to do, he simply tells them that they are free to marry anyone they wish, as long as "he belongs to the Lord"—the prerequisite of a Christian partner. There is no discussion such as, "Well, you have to find the one God has chosen for you out of all the millions of people in the world. When you find that one perfect person, then you can marry." Not at all. Paul trusts the singles in question to exercise their own good judgment and discernment in choosing a marriage partner wisely.

He tells the unmarried that "it is good" for them to stay as they are, unmarried, but unmarried couples who cannot exercise sexual self-control should marry, because it is better to marry than to burn with passion (v. 9). Again, Paul doesn't say, "It is good for you to stay as you are, unless you find the one specific person that God has picked out for you." Paul apparently has a very high view of the Corinthians' ability to choose freely. This is especially significant since the pool of eligible Christian singles in Corinth was probably not very large.

Paul tells the Corinthians that "concerning virgins I have no command of the Lord" (v. 25), that those who are engaged can marry or not marry, as they wish (v. 36), and that a widow "is free to marry anyone she wishes, only in the Lord" (v. 39 NRSV). Paul fully expects the Corinthians to use their God-given minds wisely in their decision-making and not to expect supernatural, divine guidance, even in matters as significant as choosing a marriage partner.

According to the New Testament, God is more concerned about how we treat someone we marry than whether or not we married "the right person." In life we may have lots of options; there may be many people with whom we could build a good Christian marriage. There could be many potential "right" persons. This is not to say that it doesn't matter who you marry. My life would be much different, for example, if I married a quiet, shy librarian than if my spouse was an outspoken, aggressive lawyer. Lots of important factors figure into the marriage decision.

Yet, simply put, God's will is bigger than any search for the specific "right one." Several years ago I read a story that helped me understand this. Daniel Taylor had two possibilities for a job. One was in California, the other in Minnesota. Both were good options. Both were potentially places of fruitful work and ministry. Which one was the right choice?

He wrote up a list of pros and cons. Both opportunities seemed equally attractive. He went to Scripture. He prayed. He fasted for three days. He wondered, "What if I should choose wrongly? What if I stayed in Minnesota and later found that I had missed the opportunity I had desired and that God had seemingly granted? What if I went to California and discovered that I was only returning to the safe and familiar and had ignored

God's higher call? Since I was doing my part to find God's will, why wasn't he doing his part by making it plain?"

Then a friend told him, "You're in a great position."

"How can you say that?" I asked. "I've been fasting for three days, my Bible is getting dog-eared in places it's hardly ever been opened before, I've prayed more than any time since they were handing out lottery numbers for the draft—and I'm still no closer to knowing what's the right decision."

"Listen, Dan," he replied. "You've been given a choice between two goods. You can't lose. You've got a good situation here, and you're being offered a good situation out there. I tell you, you're in great shape."

Taylor discovered that God's will was so big that he was given a choice. Either one would have been exactly where God wanted him to be. It seems that God was less concerned about whether he would take the job in Minnesota or California than about whether he was willing to serve God in either place.

"God does not economize on his blessings," Taylor writes. "His goodness multiplies itself. . . . My choices were evidence of God's munificence, not a trap to test my obedience. . . . I learned that sometimes he does not require us to make the single 'right' choice." He ends the story by saying, "I made my choice. No need to say which. It was the right choice, as would have been the other."[20]

To sum up: "Once you marry someone, that is God's choice for you. Before you marry, God has a lot of people whom he could shape to be your mate."[21]

The Problem of Passivity

3. *"If it's God's will that I'm single, there's nothing I can do about it."* Some people believe that God's will is completely foreordained: if God wants someone to be single, nothing can be done about it. One must simply be resigned to God's higher ways. While it is indeed true that God works in ways mysterious to our own understanding, it is not quite correct to conclude that we can therefore do nothing about events in our lives.

Some who hold this view have a very high view of God's sovereignty. While it is true that God is sovereign, it is incorrect to overemphasize the sovereignty of God to the exclusion of the freedom of human choice. God is all-powerful and sovereign over everything in history. At the same time, he has given us the free will to make our own choices.

One analogy that helps explain this paradox is to think of God as a sovereign ruler of a country and not as a novelist or screenwriter.

God in his role as sovereign has frequently been confused with the novelist. It is claimed that God has the ability to determine who is created, what they are like, what they will do and say, what the detailed plot is, and how it will all turn out, not just in general but for each individual.

But this is hardly an adequate view of divine sovereignty, for over whom is God sovereign? On this view he is not sovereign over creatures who can freely respond to him. Indeed, there is no real freedom in this scenario. As in the novel, the participants at best have an apparent or illusory freedom. They think that they are free and that their choices are their own. But in fact God has brought it about that they cannot but choose in a given fashion. The creation consequently turns out to be a well-orchestrated novel, deceptive at best in giving an illusion of freedom, rather than a story of divine sovereignty over responsive and responsible creatures.[22]

But, some may object, doesn't God exercise his divine power and sovereignty to determine people's lives? After all, didn't he harden Pharaoh's heart? Yes and no. Interestingly enough, if we read the Exodus narrative we will find twenty references to the hardening of Pharaoh's heart. In ten cases, it says that Pharaoh hardened his own heart. In the other ten, it says that God hardened Pharaoh's heart.[23]

The truth is really a "both/and" kind of paradox. Predestination and free will are two sides of the same coin. God presents us with opportunities, and we choose to respond one way or another. If we choose to act in ways not pleasing to God, in ways that are not in accordance with his divine character, he lets us go our own way. Pharaoh hardened his own heart, and God simply completed the task. This is what Paul says in Romans 1, where he writes that God "gave them over" to their own depravity. He did not predestine them to such a fate. He merely let them go the way they had already chosen. Our free will is especially visible in our ability to sin. "Generally God lets us make our own choices—even when they are mistakes. If you want to marry a pirate with a tattoo of a sick walrus on his forearm, don't be surprised if God lets you."[24]

But what about singleness that has not been chosen? Is God at fault for that somehow? Is this "God's will"?

We must not assume that God is to blame for our singleness any more than he is at fault for all the woes of the world. I remember a "Dear Abby" column in which a reader described a drunk driving accident that had claimed a loved one's life. She asked, "Is this God's fault or Satan's?"

Abby responded, "Leave both God and Satan out of it. The blame belongs to the drunk driver."

In the same way, we should not be too hasty to blame God when we do not know if he is at fault. The responsibility may be our own, or it may be someone else's. Or perhaps no one is at fault and our situation is simply the result of living in an imperfect world. Paul Tournier writes, "I shall never say to a woman, 'You must accept spinsterhood because it is God's will.' I do not believe that to be true. In any case, to make such an assertion is to be singularly pretentious—what do we know of God's will for other people?"[25] Tournier says that such exhortations are certainly not helpful. Something we must not do, he says, is to pretend that any state of being is willed by God.

So . . . What About Marriage?

"Is it selfish for me to want to be married?" asked Tim, age twenty-seven. "As a single, I have a lot of open time slots that I can use to serve God. But if I get married, those time slots will be used on my marriage and family, and that seems selfish. If I can serve God better as a single than as a married person, then is it wrong for me to want to get married?"

Most of us have wondered, "How can I know if God wants me to stay single or to marry? Does he have a preference?" In response, I will defer my answer to someone far more qualified to answer—John Stott. Stott is the elder statesman of evangelical Christianity in Great Britain and has been in Christian ministry for more than half a century. A superb expositor of Scripture, he is a prolific author and renowned speaker.

Now over three-quarters of a century old, Stott has spent his entire life as an unmarried person. Gary Collins has written, "It is interesting to ponder how many single seminary graduates have been encouraged by Stott's example and have persisted in finding places of service, despite the tendency in many churches to distrust and not hire single pastors. Stott no doubt has been a single mentor for many young unmarried theologians whom he has never met."[26]

In a 1975 *HIS* magazine interview, Stott was asked, "Do you think a person can know at an early age that he or she is called to singleness, or is this something you just fall into?" His reply was this:

I have no doubt there are some people who believe God has called them to be celibate and to commit themselves to celibacy for the rest of their lives. Personally I have real hesitations about the wisdom of that, because I'm not convinced that people know, say, in their early twenties, that God has called them to that. If they take a vow of celibacy, I think they may find themselves in grave difficulties later when they may fall deeply in love with somebody and begin to change their mind about their guidance. Then they're in trouble about any vow they may have taken. I'm not in favor of vows of celibacy.

I personally believe more in the second alternative you have given, that people discover it gradually and as the years pass begin to think that God is probably not calling them to marry. They don't meet a person with whom they believe God is calling them to share their life, or they don't fall deeply in love, or their work develops in such a way that it seems right for them to remain single in order to give themselves to their work rather than to a family. And as circumstances build up in this way, they begin to discern that God is calling them to be single. And that is more the situation with me.[27]

Two decades after he said this, I had the opportunity to interview John Stott myself.[28] I asked him about his views on singleness over lunch in the food court underneath the University of Michigan's student union.

Stott talked about the three grounds for singleness that Jesus mentioned in Matthew 19:12. First are those who were "born eunuchs," which Stott said would "include those with a physical defect or with a homosexual orientation. Such are congenitally unlikely to marry."

The second category are those who were made that way by others. "This would include victims of the horrible ancient practice of forcible castration. But it would also include all those today who remain single under any compulsion or external circumstance. One thinks of a daughter who feels under obligation to forego marriage in order to care for her elderly parents."[29]

The third group, those who have made themselves single for the sake of the kingdom of God, Stott defined as "people who are under no pressure from within or without, voluntarily put marriage aside, either temporarily or permanently, in order to undertake some work for the Kingdom which demands single-minded devotion." Then he spoke personally, saying that he probably falls into the third category:

In spite of rumors to the contrary, I have never taken a solemn vow or heroic decision to remain single! On the contrary, during my twenties and thirties, like most people, I was expecting to marry one day. In fact, during this period I twice began to develop a relationship with a lady who I thought might be God's choice of life partner for me. But when the time came to make a decision, I can best explain it by saying that I lacked an assurance from God that he meant me to go forward. So I drew back. And when that had happened twice, I naturally began to believe that God meant me to remain single. I'm now seventy-six and well and truly "on the shelf"! Looking back, with the benefit of hindsight, I think I know why. I could never have traveled or written as extensively as I have done if I had had the responsibilities of a wife and family.

I also asked Stott what sort of advice he would give to singles who do not have any plans at the moment but would like to marry. Stott replied:

First, don't be in too great a hurry to get married. We human beings do not reach maturity until we are about twenty-five. To marry before this runs the risk of finding yourself at twenty-five married to somebody who was a very different person at the age of twenty. So be patient. Pray daily that God will guide you to your life partner or show you if he wants you to remain single. Second, lead a normal social life. Develop many friendships. Third, if God calls you to singleness, don't fight it. Remember the key text: "Each person has his or her own gift of God's grace" (1 Cor 7:7).

Stott's answer is both profound and full of common sense. Christians need not wonder tortuously whether or not God's will for them is to remain single. Many young adults only look at the short term and panic if there are no prospects for marriage by the end of college or by age thirty. However, we ought to remember that average lifespans are much longer than they used to be. One could spend forty fruitful years as a single adult and then marry and spend another forty years in marriage. Most people who wonder if they would serve God better single or married will probably have ample opportunity to do both. Many people marry too soon and never even try to see if the single life could be fruitful for them.

Of course, this scenario of marrying later is dependent on many factors, including availability of a willing partner and age considerations if one wants to have children. But perhaps the life of Moses could serve as an example for us. Moses did not marry until age forty, began his ministry at age eighty, and died at a hundred and twenty (Acts 7:23, 30; Deut 34:7). While we may not have the same life expectancy as Moses, we still have an excellent chance to live well into our seventies, eighties or beyond. If our lives are to be that long, perhaps singles should be encouraged to remain single longer and find out what kind of effective Christian life they can have as a single. Maybe we could be the next John Stott or Mother Teresa, if only we would give God the opportunity!

Stott denies any supernatural empowerment or gifting to live the single life, but he does acknowledge a calling that is gradually discerned over time. For most of us, callings usually do not come in some dramatic, instantaneous moment like Moses at the burning bush or Paul on the Damascus road. God often progressively reveals his will to us over time. It is possible for us to gradually come to a sense of calling to be single, whether or not we ever feel God has given us any divine gifting to stay single. The mythical gift and the sense of calling are not the same, and one who has the latter should not expect the former.

Many Old Testament prophets, like Jonah or Amos, were specifically called to speak on God's behalf. This did not mean that they were given a supernatural empowerment to accomplish the task, nor were they predestined to act, like puppets on a string. In fact, at first Jonah exercised his own free will and chose not to follow the calling. It took an encounter with a fish to convince Jonah otherwise. Even so, he only followed God's call grudgingly.

A call is no guarantee of successful, triumphant living. But it does indicate a purpose to fulfill and a mission to accomplish. And while the success of the task is dependent on our obedience, God promises to be with us throughout our attempt to follow his calling.

For instance, all Christians are called to tell others about what God has done for humanity through the work of Jesus Christ. This is God's general will for all Christians. But some receive a specific calling to be witnesses in an intentional, professional way, as pastors, evangelists or missionaries. This is no guarantee that their ministries will be automatically fruitful, but God promises to be with them in the midst of their work. So too is it with a calling to singleness. All singles are called to live faithful Christian lives as singles, whether that singleness is temporary or long-term. But some may receive a special calling to remain single for some specific purpose. This may only be gradually discerned, as John Stott experienced, and in fact may not be clear except in retrospect.

Kristen, a university student, posed a different question: "When marriage is a choice, does God expect us to take it?"

Many Christians, even if they have a healthy view of the single life, feel that, given the choice, married life is somehow preferable in the eyes of God. We have already seen that God regards both singleness and marriage as equal gifts. It is worthwhile to say also that God places no obligations one way or the other. "One's decision about marriage is *regulated* and affected by the moral will of God, but *not determined* by it."[30]

God's general will is that Christians marry only other Christians. But this does not mean that a person who is offered a marriage proposal is obligated to accept it. Yoder writes, "There exists no Christian imperative to become married as soon as one can, or to prefer marriage over singleness as a more whole or wholesome situation."[31] Likewise, Grenz says, "In spite of the new status afforded singleness in the New Testament, remaining unmarried is never presented as a new law. Believers as a whole are never commanded to abstain from marrying. Even in his seemingly strong preference for the single life, Paul was careful to declare that for others to marry is no sin and that for some, marriage might even be preferable."[32]

The criteria for making the decision whether or not to marry must include consideration about whether the marriage would be a benefit or a detriment to living the Christian life. Many singles have turned down opportunities for marriage because the person was not a mature Christian, did not have similar values and priorities or did not share a common vision for ministry. It is far better to remain single than to marry a spiritually unhealthy person just for the sake of getting married.

The fact is that marriage can often dictate major life decisions. Many singles who feel a calling to serve God as missionaries overseas suddenly question that calling when a new boyfriend or girlfriend enters the picture. In pursuing the marriage, the plans to enter full-time Christian ministry fall by the wayside. Marriage itself can become an obstacle to following God's will.

Author Ed Young comments, "Marriage is not an end. It is a beginning. It is not a destination; it is a method of travel."[33] If marriage is one method of travel, singleness is the other. If we decide to marry, we are not arriving at a destination. We are simply exchanging one gift for another, one method of travel for another. And we must not believe the myth that marriage is flying first class while singleness is traveling coach. Both are equally valid methods of travel.

While many will eventually leave the single life for married life, that does not mean that marriage is for everyone any more than college (or a trip to Europe, or skill at golf) is for everyone. "Marriage is not demanded of anyone; neither is abstention from marriage, even for the sake of the kingdom of God."[34]

This is not to say that marriage should be avoided. On the contrary, John Stott (see appendix) says,

We must reject the ascetic tradition which disparages sex as legalized lust and marriage as legalized fornication. No, no. Sex is the good gift of a good Creator, and marriage is his own institution.

. . . If marriage is good, singleness is also good. It's an example of the balance of Scripture that, although Genesis 2:18 indicates that it is good to marry, 1 Corinthians 7:1 (in answer to a question posed by the Corinthians) says that "it is good for a man not to marry." So both the married and the single state are "good"; neither is in itself better or worse than the other.

Finally, we might consider that sometimes there is a reason for our singleness. It is not in any sense that God is punishing us or withholding a marriage partner from us, but perhaps God is sparing us the consequences of our own shortsightedness.

After Susan and I broke up, I came off my romantic high and realized that certain personality issues would have made our relationship very difficult, if not impossible. I was blind to those facts before, because I was so caught up in the emotion of the moment that I wouldn't let myself see. I was too eager to find somebody, too entranced by the idea of finding "the one." But in retrospect, I think what happened was that God gave me everything I was looking for in a partner, in order to show me that that wasn't right for me. What I wanted wasn't what I needed. My priorities were wrong.

I think there's real truth in the statement, "Be careful what you pray for—you just might get it." At first I thought Susan was the answer to all my prayers. It turned out that she was, but not at all in the way I expected. I wonder if God answered my prayers for that "perfect Susan" in order to show me that God knows me better than I know myself. He gave me the opportunity to date the woman of my dreams to show me that my dreams weren't big enough.

I thank God that I had the opportunity to get to know Susan. I think I'm a better person for it and that I know myself better as a result. I hope she too grew as a result of our friendship. I stopped worrying so much about "finding the right one." I'm much more concerned now about being the kind of person who lives a faithful Christian life whether I am married or single. To serve God whatever my circumstances—that is God's will for me.

Discussion Questions

1. How have you tried to discern God's leading in issues of decision-making?

2. Have you believed that God has a perfect person for you somewhere? Is it more comforting for you to believe this or to see it as a myth?

3. "It is far better to remain single than to marry an unhealthy person just for the sake of getting married." Can you think of examples of this statement?

4. If you could ask God one thing about being single, what would you ask him?

5

·····················

FREEDOM AND OPPORTUNITY

He that has wife and children hath given hostages to fortune; for they are impediments to great enterprises, either of virtue or mischief. Certainly the best works, and of greatest merit for the public, have proceeded from the unmarried or childless men, which both in affection and means have married and endowed the public.

FRANCIS BACON, "OF MARRIAGE AND SINGLE LIFE"

"**B**eing single, it's easy for me to pack up and leave on a moment's notice," Dan said. "My church was in desperate need of a male chaperone to take the high-schoolers on a weekend trip to Wisconsin. They had asked every male in the church, and no one could do it."

Dan had not planned on being a chaperone because he had a speaking engagement that Sunday. But Sam, the youth pastor, called him again and asked him if there was any possible way he could change his plans. Dan realized that if Sam took his speaking engagement for him, he would be able to make the trip. It turned out Sam had been hoping Dan would suggest that precise solution.

"At one o'clock in the afternoon I decided, 'Okay, I'll go,'" Dan recalled. "By 2:30 I was driving a van with nine kids to northern Wisconsin for the weekend!"

It soon became clear to Dan that God wanted him to be at that retreat. There Dan befriended a high-school student, also named Dan, who was a pastor's son. The younger Dan opened up to the elder Dan and confessed that he had never really made a commitment to follow Christ. Because his father was the pastor of their church, he felt like a hypocrite and had even considered suicide. Dan explained salvation to his teenage namesake and led him through a prayer of commitment to become a Christian.

"Incidentally," Dan said, "the reason the youth pastor didn't go was that he had obligations to his wife. He had promised her that he would stay and do family things that weekend."

The single life provides certain opportunities and freedoms that the married life does not have. Paul writes, in 1 Corinthians 7:32-34, "An unmarried man is concerned about the Lord's affairs—how he can please the Lord. But a married man is concerned about the affairs of this world—how he can please his wife—and his interests are divided. An unmarried woman or virgin is concerned about the Lord's affairs: Her aim is to be devoted to the Lord in both body and spirit. But a married woman is concerned about the affairs of this world—how she can please her husband." This chapter will examine some of the ways in which singles may be able to better serve God because of their singleness.

Freedom to Follow Jesus

Family-oriented churches and Christians often pity singles who seem alone, without spouses or children. However, this very situation allows Christian singles a unique opportunity to testify to the kingdom of God revealed in Jesus Christ. For the Christian single, Christian identity can take priority over all other allegiances or affiliations, whether biological, organizational or national.[1] Singles do not have the temptation of primarily thinking of ourselves as husbands, wives or parents. Instead our primary self-identity can be "followers of Jesus."

In this way, Rodney Clapp writes, the committed Christian single life can itself bear witness to the resurrection.

The single Christian ultimately must trust in the resurrection. The married, after all, can fall back on the passage of the family name to children, and on being remembered by children. But singles mount the high wire of faith without the net of children and their memory. If singles live on, it will be because there is a resurrection. And if they are remembered, they will be remembered by the family called church.[2]

The apostle Paul exemplifies this. Here is a man who, contrary to Jewish tradition and societal norm, was unmarried. As far as we know from historical records, Paul left no offspring. At his death, Christianity was no more than a fledgling religion with a handful of ragtag followers scattered across the Mediterranean. With no children to carry on his name, what were the chances that anybody would remember Paul after his death?

Though Paul had no physical children, nearly two millennia after his death, millions of Christians throughout church history know him as the apostle to the Gentiles. Millions of Bibles translated in thousands of languages across the globe name Paul as the author of one-third of the New Testament. His example as a radical follower of Christ—who did not choose a life of marriage and children—will continue to motivate the church until the time of Christ's return.

Of course, such a life is not automatic. Tim Stafford writes, "A single person is not necessarily a sign of the kingdom. If he is tangled in his longings and his sense of loss, he is not. But a single person can demonstrate with a remarkable clarity that he knows the reason he was created: to love and serve God, and him only. If that singleness of vision, that purity of heart, possesses him and shows itself in his purposeful service of others and in his preoccupation with prayer and worship, then he makes a radical statement with his life about the kingdom."[3]

In his essay "Of Marriage and Single Life," Francis Bacon wrote, "A single life doth well with churchmen, for charity will hardly water the ground where it must first fill a pool."

Certainly this is a recurring frustration for many with spouses in ministry. Many a pastor's wife has complained (as did the wife of the youth pastor in Dan's church) that her husband spends more time with the church than with his own family. This is why Paul writes, "Those who marry will face many troubles in this life, and I want to spare you this" (1 Cor 7:28). Clapp concurs. "The married must think not only of themselves and God's call for them, but also what that call will mean for spouse and children. Family does complicate things."[4]

Bluntly put, many married people in full-time ministry either shouldn't be in ministry or shouldn't be married. Richard Foster writes, "One of the great tragedies of our day is the number of Christian leaders who have given themselves unselfishly to the cause of Christ, but have destroyed their marriages and their children in the process. And it was all so unnecessary. Many of them simply needed to understand that their sense of call was incompatible with the responsibilities of marriage, and to choose the single life."[5]

In contrast to the married person, who by necessity must be concerned with the needs of spouse and family, Foster says that "the single person can concentrate with abandon on the advancement of the Kingdom of God. . . . Paul was not against marriage, but he did insist that people should count the cost. No one should enter the covenant of marriage without understanding the immense amount of time and energy involved in making that relationship work. We need to face the fact that we cannot do many of the kinds of things which Paul did and be married."[6]

A primary advantage of singleness is a mobility that many married people envy. With the responsibilities of a spouse and children comes the idea that it may be best to settle down more or less permanently, in order to provide children with a community to grow up in and a place to call home. Of course it is true that many married people do move across the country frequently due to job changes and corporate transfers. But the married who move must consider the effects of the move on the other members of the family, while a single person may not have as many such concerns.

As John Stott says, the liberty of singleness is that "single people experience the great joy of being able to devote themselves, with concentration and without distraction, to the work of the Lord."[7]

Stafford writes, "[Jesus and Paul] were celibate because their singleness enabled them to serve God in a way that would otherwise have been impossible. . . . A good spouse must give first priority to his family; he cannot easily be radical while raising children."[8]

Unfortunately, many churches have precisely the opposite view of singleness. Because churches tend to be family-oriented, they often limit their consideration of pastors and church leaders to those who are married. Most churches want a pastor with a spouse and kids, believing that they will be better able to relate to couples and families. Sadly, that means that these churches wouldn't hire Jesus or Paul.

Qualified single adults are passed over because it is believed that their single state means that something must be wrong with them. Single adults are viewed as immature or naive, unable to understand the issues of marriages and families.

Try being a single minister today, and the vocation options are few or limited. Oh, most churches probably won't admit they favored Marvin Married over Stuart Single because of marital status, but the issue is always there. I know one seminary classmate who recently was a candidate for a staff position. In his early forties and never married, he was never really given serious consideration, although he was qualified for the job. Some feared he might play around too much with other singles in the church. There's also the unarticulated suspicion that he might be gay. The single male at top leadership levels in the church is suspect.[9]

Churches can be similarly biased against laypersons who are single. Some churches disallow singles from being elders or deacons. Church boards almost always consist of married people (usually men). "One church I know is probably more willing to place a divorced single on its board than a never-married single."[10]

As justification for marginalizing singles, some churches cite 1 Timothy 3:2-5 and Titus 1:6, which say that an elder must be "the husband of but one wife" and "must manage his own family well and see that his children obey him with proper respect." Singles are not allowed to have leadership roles, it is claimed, because somebody must know how to "manage his own family" before he is able to "take care of God's church."

This view misapplies Scripture. Commentator William Hendriksen says about 1 Timothy 3:2, "This cannot mean that an overseer or elder must be a married man. Rather, *it is assumed* that he is married—as was generally the case—and it is stipulated that in this marital relationship he must be an example to others of faithfulness to his one and only marriage partner."[11] These verses condemn not singleness but polygamy. Paul presupposes that most of those aspiring to be elders would already be married, and he is stating that they must be married to only one wife, not two or three. Also in view here is a condemnation of adultery and a call to marital faithfulness for those who are married. But Paul makes no statement that one who is not married cannot serve in church leadership. After all, such a statement would be self-contradictory—he would disqualify himself!

Furthermore, the logic of Paul's argument is *not* that being a good parent is a prerequisite for being a good church leader. Paul only cites the negative: "If anyone does not know how to manage his own family, how can he take care of the church?" (1 Tim 3:5). The argument is from the lesser to the greater—one who is not a good parent would not be a good church leader. Managing the church is the model for managing the family, not vice versa. The church is the first family, and the biological family is secondary. We do not apply family models to the church; we apply church models to the family.

What churches or other prospective employers should keep in mind is the fact that marriage is no guarantee of good character. Integrity is not dependent on marital status. A single may or may not be more prone to sexual temptation than a married person. Simply because leaders are married does not mean that they are better qualified to face temptation. After all, many pastors have affairs even though they have spouses.

Perhaps the bias against singles in church leadership could be resolved by a better view of pastoral ministry. Instead of looking to one pastor to understand and connect with the needs of the majority of the congregation, a healthier approach would be to have a pastoral team of people in many different life situations who could connect with different populations in the church. Such a team would include people who are male and female, older and younger, married and single. Perhaps then churches could see that singles can serve God in ways that others cannot.

Dan Harrison describes the work of a young single named Ricardo.[12] During college, Ricardo's girlfriend, Jennifer, spent a summer in inner-city Los Angeles working with an urban ministry. She challenged Ricardo to go on a spring-break trip to L.A. with the same ministry. Ricardo did, and he was so moved by the issues of racism and injustice that he returned for the entire summer. There he was robbed of expensive belongings, including his camera, CD player and notebook computer. He came to grips with his own racism. And a pastor from South Africa asked him to think about justice as a global issue. In response, Ricardo moved to Soweto, working for racial reconciliation across ethnic and denominational lines in South Africa.

One would expect that Ricardo and Jennifer, like most college couples, would get married soon after graduation. Not so. "We've been dating for four years now," Ricardo said. "I would love to be married, but she has lots more to see before settling down."

Harrison notes, "Jennifer is currently working in a refugee camp in northern Thailand and thinks her next stop will be Amsterdam. Prior to that she was in Russia."

As singles, Ricardo and Jennifer have the opportunity and the freedom of mobility to travel and serve all around the world. Of course, they could have chosen to work together overseas as a married couple. The point, however, is that both Ricardo and Jennifer chose their priorities in light of serving God. Their ultimate concern was to be in places where they could actively minister and help accomplish God's work and purposes on earth. And as inviting and appealing as marriage might be, they understood that some things in life are more important than getting married. Ricardo said, "I know I'm where I belong right now, and you couldn't tear me away from this place."

Freedom to Show God's Love

Ellen helped direct her church's children's Christmas musical. During the rehearsals, she built relationships with all the different children. She noticed that she was better able to interact with the whole group than the married women, who paid special attention to their own children.

"I think being single has helped me try to love all the kids equally," she said. "If I had a child of my own in the play, I might have shown him or her preferential treatment or been biased one way or another. I might have neglected other kids because my own was there. But this way, they're all 'my kids,' and I'm sensitive to treat them all fairly."

Stanley Grenz has observed that in Christian community, singles and marrieds together testify to God's amazing love for humanity. They do so in different but complementary ways.

The married person models God's love through his or her marriage relationship, demonstrating exclusivity. The married person pledges fidelity and faithfulness to the spouse alone. This reflects how God loves us and commits himself to us in wholehearted, complete devotion. God loves us with the jealous love of a lover.

But married love, by its very nature, is self-limiting. The marital relationship requires total, undivided commitment and investment of great amounts of time and energy to make it work. Married people are often limited in their ability to build outside relationships because of responsibilities to the spouse and family.

However, the single has no such limitations. By not having a spouse, a single is free to build many relationships with many people. In this way, the single adult is an example of the fact that God loves all people, not just a few. While married Christians emulate God's *exclusive* love, single Christians demonstrate God's *nonexclusive* love. "The single life provides powerful imagery of the universal, nonexclusive and expanding nature of God's love," Grenz writes. "The loving God is always seeking the outsider so that still more persons can enjoy the divine fellowship. Singleness portrays this dynamic."[13]

As Grenz writes, "Marriage expresses the divine will to form a close community of fellowship on the basis of exclusive love and fidelity to covenant. The single life, in contrast, represents the expansive nature of the divine love that seeks to encompass all of humanity in the relationship of community."[14]

Writer and poet Kathleen Norris spent two extended residencies at a Benedictine monastery and observed how monks and nuns lived the celibate life. She found that "celibacy was a part of their being such terrific people." The monks described their celibacy as a form of freedom; they told her, "I am so much more free than I could be if I had gotten married, or if I were not in this monastery." Norris came to realize that "there's a kind of paradox where commitment to celibacy . . . can open you to other people because you're secure in a commitment, which allows you a great freedom and a great openness to other people." Observing the celibates helped Norris understand herself and the nature of her marriage relationship better, precisely because it displayed a commitment to share God's love in a way that marital love could not.[15]

Norris found that many members of the community spoke of celibacy as helping them build relationships and love others. One nun spoke of celibacy as a freedom, "freedom to love many people without being unfaithful to any of them." Another said that celibacy stretches the ability to love, particularly to love nonexclusively. The nuns helped her see, she says, "that a non-sexually-active love can be just as passionate and just as absorbing as a genitally rooted one, and that such a love has as its center the idea of being fully focused and intentional."[16]

Some nuns spoke of a celibate philosophy that "loves all" and "loves all well." This speaks of the "generative" qualities of celibacy. "We're not making babies," one sister says, "but we can make relationships." Another nun agreed, "To be celibate, it seems to me, means first of all being a loving person in a way that frees you to serve others. Otherwise celibacy has no point."[17]

Mother Teresa is an example of how a single person can demonstrate God's love for the world. Hardly anyone, Protestant or Catholic, Christian or not, would not speak highly of Mother Teresa. But Tim Stafford reminds us that fundamentally Mother Teresa is a human being who happens to be single. Single-minded in her dedication and commitment, she has accomplished a ministry with extraordinary impact, showing God's extravagant love for the world's poorest and most unfortunate.

"It is very difficult to imagine any married person calling the world to account in quite her way," Stafford says. "Celibacy removes the barriers marriage puts up to spontaneous love of God and neighbor."[18]

Freedom to Experience Personal Growth

Many single young adults today are able to take advantage of enriching opportunities to further their education, to travel or to do things that they would not otherwise have the freedom to do. After graduating from college, it is not unusual for adults in their twenties to postpone pursuing a career while they spend a year backpacking across Europe.

Part of this trend is a shift in views toward work.[19] A career used to be considered an end in itself. A person could graduate from college and go straight into a job with a reasonable expectation of staying with the same company for an entire career, retiring as a company man or woman. This is no longer the case. Barna writes that while boomers have seen work as an end in itself and a key source of personal identity, Xers view work only as a means to an end.[20]

Because of minimal job security, today's young adults tend not to invest their energies and identities in their jobs. Contrary to media portrayal, Xers are not slackers—they just seem that way when compared with workaholic boomers. Boomers live to work, while Xers work to live.[21] Xers reject the yuppie ethic of workaholism. Climbing the corporate ladder is seen as selfish and futile. Good jobs are in short supply, so many young adults find themselves underemployed, working in fields unrelated to their interests. Entry-level work tends to be unchallenging and meaningless. One friend told me that some days he spends about half an hour actually working and the remainder of the day reading computer manuals and playing cards. During one forty-two-hour work week, he logged a total of fifty minutes of actual work—not because he was lazy, but simply because he was not given any work to do.

Xers see work only as a means to an end, a necessary evil to earn money needed to sustain life and to fund other more meaningful pursuits, such as art, music, ministry or community service. Rock-climbing, travel, cultural events—these are what life is about, not pushing papers at a desk from nine to five.

For this reason, many Xers find themselves taking what is called an "antisabbatical." An antisabbatical is defined as "a job taken with the sole intention of staying only for a limited period of time (often one year). The plan is usually to raise enough funds to partake in another, more personally meaningful activity such as watercolor sketching in Crete or designing computer-knit sweaters in Hong Kong. Employers are rarely informed of the plan."[22]

Singles can use antisabbaticals in a way that married people can't. A married couple is expected to sink roots into a community, especially if they have children. They lack the mobility to up and leave. Furthermore, financial resources must often be allocated to the needs of the family and cannot be as easily invested in special trips and educational experiences.

The adventures available to singles need not be used for purely personal interests. They can be of great benefit to others. Many give time to charitable organizations, such as soup kitchens and homeless shelters. Others volunteer with groups like Habitat for Humanity. Since institution of the Peace Corps in 1961 by John F. Kennedy, more than 140,000 people have volunteered for service in education, environment, health, business and agriculture. In 1995, 6,858 volunteers served in ninety-seven countries. Of these, 93 percent were single.[23]

Many Christian singles have gone on short-term missions trips all over the world. Heather, a nurse, has been on several medical missionary trips to Honduras and the Dominican Republic, as well as spending a summer in inner-city Indianapolis. Shelley has volunteered with churches in Mexico. Amy worked with an orphanage in Romania. Dan spent a year in Belgium. Ellen toured with a music ministry across the southwestern United States and Hawaii. Cheryl has been on trips to Russia and the Ukraine.

Higher education is another venue for personal advancement that many singles pursue. Because of increasing numbers of college graduates, a four-year degree no longer has the value it once did. In order to increase their marketability, many young adults are going on to graduate school.

Singles can spend their time away from work pursuing personal interests instead of expending further energy on family concerns. "A single person is freer to expend his or her nurturing energy on the job. The helping professions, especially, require an enormous output of the same emotional energy needed for supporting a spouse and children. A single person who has dealt with needy people all day will not usually have to come home to another set of people demanding attention and support."[24]

Sometimes singles become accustomed to having such freedom and find it to be a stumbling block when they marry. Smith writes,

> Many who marry in their college or high school years, and some who marry well into adulthood, discover that they are not nearly as ready to let go of the advantages of singleness as they thought. Though the prospect of marriage was alluring, once the newness wears off they find themselves restless and longing for the freedom of movement they enjoyed before becoming attached. Not a few marriages break up over this tension.[25]

The lesson for singles who enjoy the freedom of mobility is to be cautious with prospects for marriage. Engaged couples should work through issues of independence and personal freedom well before the wedding. Blending two lives into a marriage is by no means automatic or simple. If one person is set on maintaining the same level of freedom he or she enjoyed as a single while the prospective spouse is not, problems may be imminent.

Freedom to Find Healing and Wholeness

"One of the good things about being single longer is that it can help you grow up more," said Nick, age thirty-one. "I know that if I had been married five years ago I would be a much different person than I am now." Nick now has a sense of personal security and internal strength that he didn't have several years ago. If he had married five years ago, he might have done so with the hope of gaining a sense of security from his spouse. Now that he has a greater sense of wholeness, he is free to pursue healthy relationships instead of looking for security in another person.

Not only do singles have the opportunity to pursue a wide breadth of activities, they can also pursue depth in emotional, psychological and spiritual growth. Singles have the opportunity to develop their own personal identity apart from a marriage partner.

Many singles need to find healing, wholeness and recovery from past hurts. Today's young adults are the first generation to grow up in daycare centers. They are children of divorce, latchkey kids and victims of abuse of many kinds. These singles must come to grips with who they are as individuals and work through issues of past brokenness.

"Because of my parents' divorce," one single said, "I wondered if there were behavior patterns in me—in the way I interacted with people—that would kill me in relationships, that would totally ruin a marriage. I thought of it as a ticking time bomb—something within me that would emerge and turn me into a horrible monster. Over the course of time I realized, yeah, there might be those things inside of me. But if I take steps to follow God, God will take care of those things."

One problem with many marriages is that one or both partners bring past woundedness and dysfunction into the marriage. They have issues that have never been dealt with; they did not get themselves healthy before entering into the marriage. Many singles should hold off consideration of marriage until they find healing and wholeness for themselves as individuals.

Because of past hurts, many singles view themselves as a half in search for a missing other half. The most they can offer a prospective mate is only half a person, not a whole being who is complete and whole as an individual in Christ. Marriage counselor Neil Clark Warren says, "A great marriage requires two healthy people, and the time to get healthy is before you get married."[26]

Many young marrieds jump from their parents' house to an apartment with their newfound spouse with barely any time in between to learn how to stand on their own. As a result, the marriages are weaker. The divorce rate for twenty-one- and twenty-two-year olds is twice as high as it is for twenty-four- and twenty-five-year-olds.[27] Many marital problems could be prevented if people were in less of a rush to get married.

The experience of living alone develops survival skills that help avoid marrying for the wrong reasons. . . . By affirming the single person and respecting his or her decision to live independently and perhaps never marry, many ill-fated marriages could be avoided. If young people need to get away from a difficult home situation, it is better for them to live on their own than to use marriage as an escape. As difficult as it may be to strike out on one's own, it is far better for a young person to leave a troubled home, live independently, and spend time alone sorting out the conflicts than it is to transfer all the past problems to a new home by getting married at the first opportunity.[28]

In this respect, being single does not mean that one is unattractive or has failed to find a willing partner. It is rather a level-headed choice to stand on one's own and to take care of personal issues and problems before entering marriage. In fact, an unmarried person may have had various opportunities for marriage but turned them down because the other person was not healthy enough for a lifelong commitment. We should not say, "What's wrong with her?" Rather, we should say, "Good for her. Far better to break things off now than to marry him and get into all sorts of trouble later."

Paul Tournier writes:

The spinster feels that people suspect her of having failed to marry because of her complexes. . . . But many other women have remained celibate because they have quite freely refused some proposal of marriage which they could not have accepted without devaluing themselves in their own eyes. All honor to them—that is a sign of health, not psychological sickness.[29]

In discussing widows, Paul writes in 1 Corinthians 7:39-40 that a widow is free to remarry if she wishes, as long as her intended husband is a Christian. But he also says, "But in my judgment she is more blessed if she remains as she is" (NRSV). Paul says that singleness can be a state of blessedness, not only in the sense that singles can be vehicles of God's blessing to other people, but also that they themselves receive blessing from God by finding personal identity in Christ and relying upon him. The result can be a stronger Christian identity, a healthier personality and a more secure perspective on life.

Freedom to Marry

Singles have one freedom in particular that married people do not have. Clapp writes, "Single Christians, ironically, are also our most vivid witnesses to the *freedom to marry*. The ancient Israelites were not free to remain single. Singleness, in a real way, was synonymous with death and extinction. But we are now truly free to be single, and so truly free to be married. . . . If we are not truly free to be single, we are not truly free to be married."[30]

Western singles often forget how free our society is for single adults. While there are still big challenges in living as a single adult in American society, they are nothing compared to those in cultures where the only single men are criminals and the only single women are prostitutes. Our American culture affords individuals the choice either to marry or to remain single. The freedom of choice gives value to both states. Neither is an automatic, inevitable situation. Marriage is entered into freely, not under coercion.

Many married people would love to be in a single person's shoes again. In fact, this may be one reason why adultery and divorce are so prevalent. Married people, dissatisfied with their marriage partners, want to be free to find someone new. Singles may forget to value the opportunity they have to date different people and venture into new relationships without the binding commitment of marriage.

Singles who have a healthy view of their singleness can, in the long run, produce healthier marriages:

> If without teaching celibacy as a permanent obligation we teach it as a present preference, the overall social effect will be more mature marriages of couples who are better matched, more experienced, better educated, less compulsive about getting married, more ready for parenthood, less likely to have too many children, and more respectful of singles.[31]

"I would like to be married," Hans said, "but I would much rather be single and wish I was married than be married and wish I was single." In this sense, singleness is a better place to be than marriage. For a single person there is open-endedness, with the possibility and potential for finding a marriage partner. For married people who believe in the lifelong permanence of the marriage vow, such an option no longer exists.

Gary Collins writes of those who voluntarily choose singleness: "These singles face many of the problems that concern all unmarried people, but those who have chosen to postpone marriage often have a healthy outlook. For them singleness is not seen as a tragedy that has come as the result of unwanted circumstances. Instead singleness is viewed as a choice that can be changed later."[32]

Koons and Anthony state, "Numerous studies indicate that the most contented married persons were those who had not rushed into marriage to escape an unhappy home or loneliness as a single, but had first established a sense of well-being and happiness as an individual."[33]

The Freedom of Childlessness

Being free from caring for children is not the situation of all singles, since many are single parents, and it also applies to married couples who have no children. Childlessness can be a freedom and opportunity just as singleness is. "Nowhere has it been shown that life satisfaction is based on the presence of children in the home. In fact, most sociologists agree that shortly after the birth of the first child in a home there is a decrease in marital satisfaction. This decrease tends to continue until shortly after the children become fairly independent young adults. The return of maximum happiness comes after the departure of the last child!"[34]

Married couples would do well to remember that having children is an option, not a societal obligation. Couples can choose to remain childless as an expression of "married celibacy":

> It would be fruitful to examine . . . the commitment of a couple to child-lessness, not on the grounds of ease or materialism, but for the sake of mobility and concentration of ministry. A permanent commitment of a couple to childlessness would in some ways be analogous to the commitment of celibacy.[35]

Couples without children, whether by choice or by circumstance, can find opportunities for ministry and outreach that they might not have time for if they were rearing their own children. It is true that couples who desire children may experience real pain when faced with infertility. This pain should not be minimized. However, just as singles can view their singleness as an opportunity instead of a deficit, so too can childless couples view their situation as a gift. Couples who are unable to have children of their own can adopt and in so doing provide a home for a child who otherwise might have been aborted.

Those without children need not be consumed with worry about abuse at daycare centers or the quality of their children's education. Free from the anxieties of parenting, they can invest their time and emotional energies elsewhere, especially in community service and the life of the church. Money that otherwise would be allocated for their kids' college educations can be used to fund ministries and charities.

Richard Foster describes a couple who voluntarily chose childlessness for ministry purposes. He writes, "I am very close to a couple who have consciously chosen not to have children so that they may have a more effective ministry among teenagers. Their home is open to young and old day and night. Although one night in their home is enough to drive me crazy, I must confess that their ministry is an extraordinarily effective one."[36]

I think of one of my college professors, Chris, and his wife, Cathy. This couple in their mid-thirties have no children and do not plan to have any. Some of my best memories of college are of this professor playing volley-ball with us students, staying overnight with us at a college retreat and holding chess tournaments. He's one of the best-loved professors at my college, primarily because he invests the time to interact with students more than other professors. I remember his telling me, "We may not have any kids of our own, but we see all of you students as 'our kids.'"

Modern Christians practice "biological church growth"—expansion of the church by physical procreation and reproduction. But Jerome advised fourth-century Christians not to have children, arguing that instead of spending time rearing our own children, Christians should look for opportunities to bring non-Christians into the church and produce "spiritual offspring" rather than biological. If we were not so concerned about our own biological families, we could invest more time and energy in outreach and evangelism. This worldview suggests that some other concerns are just as important and valuable as marriage or children.

"I have learned to be content whatever the circumstances," Paul writes. "I know what it is to be in need, and I know what it is to have plenty. I have learned the secret of being content in any and every situation, whether well fed or hungry, whether living in plenty or in want" (Phil 4:11-12). We too can find contentedness regardless of our marital status. Whether we are single or married, whether we have children or not, we ought to see the opportunities that any situation in life may have for us. We can choose to view our situations optimistically, as filled with potential for fruitful Christian living.

Discussion Questions

1. What freedoms do you think of when you think of singleness?
2. In what ways does your life give testimony to Christ's resurrection?
3. Do you find that churches limit singles' opportunities to serve? Can you find a new way to serve in your own church or in another ministry?
4. What opportunities have you had as a single to share God's nonexclusive love?
5. Have you taken opportunities to find personal growth or healing?
6. "I'd rather be single and wish I was married than married and wish I was single." Is this statement true for you?

6

....

FROM LONELINESS
TO SOLITUDE

Rachel: "Monica just broke my seashell lamp!"
Chandler: "Neat! I'm gonna die alone!"
Rachel: [pause] "Okay, you win."
FRIENDS

In an episode of the TV show *Friends*, crotchety neighbor Mr. Heckles dies and leaves everything to "the two noisy girls in the apartment above mine," Monica and Rachel. As the six friends go through Heckles's apartment, they discover memorabilia that includes Heckles's old high-school yearbook. They find out that Heckles was class clown, played the clarinet in band and was extremely picky about the women he dated—just like Chandler.

Chandler goes into a personal crisis because he sees that Heckles's finicky dating habits kept him single all his life. Heckles kept pictures of women he dated with comments about why he rejected them: "too tall," "big gums," "too loud," "too smart," "makes noise when she eats."

"This is me!" Chandler exclaims. "This is what I do! I'm going to end up alone, just like he did!"

"C'mon, Heckles was a nutcase," Joey reassures Chandler.

"Our trains are on the same track, okay?" Chandler responds. "Yeah, sure, I'm coming up thirty years behind him, but the stops are all the same! Bittertown! Aloneville! Hermit Junction!"

In desperation to *not* become like Heckles, Chandler calls up Janice, the ex-girlfriend he dumped three times before. She shows up married and pregnant. Chandler freaks. He bemoans to his friends, "Janice was my safety net! Now I have to get a snake!"

"Why is that?" Phoebe asks.

"If I'm going to be an old lonely man, I'm gonna need a thing! You know, a hook! Like that guy on the subway who eats his own face! I'll be Crazy Man with a Snake! Crazy Snake Man! And I'll get more snakes and call them my babies! Kids won't walk past my place—they'll run! Run away from Crazy Snake Man!"[1]

This kind of catastrophic reaction is an extreme example of the fear of loneliness. For Chandler, the worst thing that can possibly happen is that he will grow old and die alone. He fears the day when all of his other friends will be married and have families, and he will be left alone at holidays. Chandler believes that he needs a spouse in order to have a happy, meaningful life, and he believes that to end up alone is to be a failure in life. While Chandler's feelings are funny because they are so extreme, many singles resonate with his concerns. *Am I going to die alone?* we wonder. *What if I never find anybody?*

Loneliness Is Not Aloneness

We must make an important distinction. *Aloneness* is the physical state of being separated from other people. *Loneliness* is an emotional state of feeling disconnected from other people, a sense of being alone and yearning to be in relationship with others.[2] Loneliness is not directly dependent on the presence of people. One can be alone and not be lonely. On the other hand, one can be surrounded by people and still feel very lonely.

"Aloneness is the recognition of being apart. Loneliness is the painful feeling of separation from an unacceptability to others. . . . Loneliness is not a condition of physical isolation, but a state of mind."[3] Helena Wilkinson describes the state of loneliness as "not just a matter of being unattached, but feeling unattached."[4]

Often our response to loneliness is to try to escape it. During a class on spirituality, a student gave a report on a book that dealt with the issue of loneliness. She began her presentation by asking us, "What do you do when you're lonely?"

The answers around the room were fairly normal. "Turn on the radio." "Call a friend." "Go shopping." "Watch TV." "Read a book." "Write a letter." "Mope around, pout and feel sorry for myself."

The student acknowledged these responses with a knowing nod. Then she said, "When we're lonely, we look for distractions."

The truth of that statement struck me. Most of us seek distractions to keep from being lonely. We fill our schedules with events; we immerse ourselves in work; we distract ourselves with television or medicate our pain by chemical and substance abuse. Richard Foster writes, "Our fear of being alone drives us to noise and crowds."[5] But loneliness is not solved by immersing ourselves in activities or having people around.

Our personality type is a factor in how we approach being alone. Some people are extroverts and are energized by interacting with people. They find aloneness unnatural and uncomfortable. For this reason, extroverts tend to escape isolation by finding people and events to fill their schedules: people to see, things to do. This bustle of activity, however, may continue to mask a lonely heart.

Introverts, on the other hand, tend to be drained by too much interaction with people and find refreshment and renewal in time alone. Aloneness may then be less threatening. However, the risk for some introverts is isolation and introspection. Individuals who are shy and alone a lot may conclude that people don't want to be with them. Then the state of aloneness turns into feelings of loneliness.

In fact, loneliness may have nothing to do with singleness. "We need to understand where our loneliness comes from—to realize that the cause of our loneliness could be far greater than simply being single."[6] Our feelings of loneliness could come from issues of abandonment or disconnectedness we suffered in childhood, or they could be rooted in traumas we experienced later in life. Or the cause could be spiritual—our sense of loneliness may be the result of a lack of relationship with God.

Whatever the cause, we must recognize that singleness itself does not cause loneliness. There is no direct relationship between the two. After all, many married people are lonely, and many singles are not. Perhaps loneliness is an occupational hazard of singleness, just as materialism is a hazard of working in a shopping mall. The single life is a yard in which the crabgrass of loneliness is prone to grow. We must simply do what we can to keep the weeds from cropping up.

Rethinking Our Assumptions

In order to counter loneliness, we must ask ourselves, "What does it *mean* to be alone?" Does being alone mean that we are miserable, or does it mean that we are free? Whether we realize it or not, we attach meanings to the situations in which we find ourselves. We carry unspoken mental assumptions that cause us to feel one way or another about the situations of life. Counselors call this "self-talk."

For example, being alone may simply be an objective fact and carry the self-talk message *I am alone. Nobody else is with me right now. No big deal.* However, we can also attach negative connotations to aloneness. In that case, being alone can mean *I am alone because people don't like to be with me. I am unlovable. I am undesirable. I am a social failure. I am a bad person. Nobody could ever want to be with me.* Mere aloneness gives way to loneliness if we believe these kinds of messages.

Once we identify such negative messages, we must ask ourselves, *Are these thoughts true?* We subconsciously give ourselves self-talk all the time, whether we recognize it or not. We need to stop ourselves, listen carefully to the internal messages we are giving ourselves and identify whether or not they are true.

If my self-talk statement is *Nobody wants to be with me,* I must ask myself, *Is this true?* Do people really abhor my presence? Do they run out the door screaming when I approach? Probably not. But if I sense that people are not particularly interested in striking up conversations with me, I must ask myself why. Perhaps I have bad breath. Maybe I don't take enough initiative to interact with others. Maybe I'm just too shy, and nobody notices me. Or perhaps my personality type clashes with theirs.

Another unspoken assumption is the belief *I am not a whole person unless I have a partner or spouse.* Whether we ever say so out loud or not, many of us feel incomplete as single persons.

One love song has lyrics that say that the singer "can't go on" if he's on his own, without somebody to call his own. Though I've heard the song many times before, one day I heard it again on the car radio. This time, I challenged the statement.

"Is that true?" I asked my radio. "Is it true that this guy won't be able to survive life without his lover? Of course not! He'll get over her soon enough and forget he ever cared for her! What a crock! What a lie! This song is false!" (I actually said this out loud to my radio. Good thing I was alone in the car at the time.)

We must recognize that *loneliness is not solved by marriage.* Somebody who is lonely when single will probably still be lonely when married. People are often lonely in marriage because they were lonely as singles. Perhaps they saw marriage as the solution to loneliness, not realizing that they needed to deal with the issue of their own personal loneliness. They never cultivated an internal sense of wholeness and healthy solitude. This is not to say that being happy by yourself is a prerequisite for a good marriage. However, all of us—single or married—need to have a sense of identity with Christ that doesn't depend on our relationships with other people. Otherwise, a marriage partner is no more than a distraction that masks our inner emptiness.

Behind some of our assumptions may lie the belief that we don't deserve to be lonely. In this age of entitlement, many of us grew up without having to work very hard for various benefits in life. We have come to believe that we are somehow entitled to a life without loneliness or even entitled to a dating partner or spouse. We must recognize that we have no real basis for any such sense of entitlement.

I was reminded of this when I read about the experiences of author Gerald Sittser, who lost his wife, mother and four-year-old daughter in a car accident. In coming to grips with the loss, he realized: "Granted, I did not deserve to lose three members of my family. But then again, I am not sure that I deserved to have them in the first place. . . . Perhaps I did not deserve their deaths; but I did not deserve their presence in my life either."[7] Sittser recognized that his family members were an undeserved blessing and gift from God. Though he suffers loss that he does not deserve, he also receives mercy and grace that he does not deserve.

Singles can learn from Sittser's example. We must not have false expectations that God will provide a person for us to spend our lives with. Nor should we feel any sense of entitlement, that we somehow "deserve" to not be alone. God never promised us that.

Loss of Community

After graduating from college, John took a public relations job in a monastery located in a rural town. He discovered he didn't like being in a small town where there were few people his age. After a year, he went to graduate school.

John found graduate school interesting, but he found it hard to meet people with common interests. He discovered that it was much more difficult to make friends than in college. Social life was no longer as available. He tried joining a small group but found that the members had little in common and lacked connectedness. He had no sense of community.

Many singles feel the same disorientation that John experienced after college. During college, community is built in. We are immersed in a sea of people our age, and it isn't too hard to find people with similar likes and tastes.

Life after graduation can be quite a shock. Like the Israelites in the wilderness, who wanted to go back to Egypt, recent graduates often look back to college with nostalgia. They begin to miss having those noisy neighbors down the hall, even though they hindered studies and sleep. At least they were there. At least one could walk into the cafeteria and find a friend to eat with. You can't do that now when you go to McDonald's. Now you sit by yourself.

Students who marry right after graduation may not immediately notice this postcollegiate shift. Their main concern is adjusting to marriage and living with a spouse. Like singles, these couples still lose the immediate contact with the masses of people, but that fact is not recognized because a young married couple does not think of themselves as alone. They think of themselves as together.

The fact is that newlywed life can be very lonely. One woman told me about getting married shortly after graduation. She worked while her husband went to seminary. Their schedules limited their time together. One day, as she came home from work to an empty house, she suddenly realized just how alone she was. She asked herself, *Is this what I got married for?*

Sometimes the newlyweds blame each other, thinking that they have lost their friends because their spouse is monopolizing all their time. That is not really the case. They simply graduated from college and lost the sense of being surrounded by a community, and this would have happened whether they had married or not. It might take marrieds awhile to notice post-collegiate isolation; singles usually recognize it immediately.

One reason why singles struggle with loneliness is that we never fully grieve the loss of community. At transition points, like graduations and moves, we experience loss. Here are some postcollegiate losses that need to be processed and mourned.

Loss of familiarity. After four or more years at college, you have a real sense of home. You know the best restaurants in town and the cheapest movie theaters. Whether you enjoyed your college experience or not, the location has become a part of your history. It is no mistake that alumni refer to their college as their *alma mater*—Latin for "nourishing mother." College, for many of us, is really like an adoptive parent. When we graduate, we leave our adoptive "second nest," and the passage is as significant as leaving childhood.

Loss of status. At our alma mater, we fit into certain niches. We belonged to organizations and participated in activities. After several years in the choir or serving as a campus fellowship leader, we had gained some status. Younger students looked to us for direction and leadership. Now we're no longer a student council officer or a Resident Assistant. Nobody cares what we did in college. That coveted status position is now nothing more than a line on the résumé.

Loss of intimacy. The close friends we spent all those years with are now nowhere nearby. Just before I graduated, seven of us went on a senior class trip. After graduation, three stayed in Minnesota, two went to Tennessee, one went back to New Zealand, and I went to Illinois. It was quite a blow to realize that the seven of us may never again be gathered together in this lifetime. While I still try to keep in touch with my friends, we no longer have the strong sense of intimate closeness that we had when we all went to school together.

These three losses are part of the postcollegiate loss of community. Movies like *St. Elmo's Fire* and *Reality Bites* depict the difficulties that we have adjusting to these losses. And they are legitimate losses that need to be grieved and processed. But this is something that many singles never do.

For some young adults, the entry to the postcollegiate world is so traumatic that they experience what Douglas Coupland calls a "mid-twenties breakdown," which he defines as "a period of mental collapse occurring in one's twenties, often caused by an inability to function outside of school or structured environments coupled with a realization of one's essential aloneness in the world."[8]

The 1994 movie *The Shawshank Redemption* was about the lives of prisoners in a New England penitentiary. One of the characters was an old convict named Brooks, who had spent fifty years in Shawshank. When notified of his impending release, Brooks, terrified at the thought of returning to the outside world, threatened to stab a fellow inmate. He felt the need to commit some sort of crime that would enable him to return to the prison. "Here, he's the librarian," his friend Red observed. "He's somebody important, educated. Out there, he probably wouldn't even be able to get a library card." After his release, Brooks tried to adjust to society, but ultimately was unable to function away from his life in the prison. He had become what Red called "institutionalized."

Many of today's young adults have become institutionalized, not in prison, but in school. After thirteen years of education from kindergarten to twelfth grade and another four or more years of college or other higher education, young adults have become institutionalized into the educational culture. Outside the institution, loneliness can strike.

Sometimes we are lonely because we have never fully grieved the loss of community. Walter Wangerin writes that life is filled with "little deaths" that we need to mourn and grieve, and one of these deaths is displacement. At every transition and every time we move, we experience a grief that is entirely legitimate:

[When people move,] they uproot themselves; they break or strain or stretch the countless filaments of relationships in which they had lived all the years they dwelt in this neighborhood, this city or state.

We are woven into communities, though we may be unconscious of the webbing that supports us—the shopkeepers, neighbors, church families—until we move to another town. And then we become terribly conscious, because of the breaking. A thousand tiny *snaps!*

Should anyone wonder, then, why even the happy move that one had planned for can cause such mortal grief? *As if someone had died,* we whisper, bewildered, believing that all the old friendships will last. *We'll write and visit each other still. And there are good people here to receive us. Yet—* Well, now you know: someone did die. You, at displacement. And the period of distress, the overwhelming sense of vulnerability and loneliness and even the heavy lethargy that follows, are natural after all.[9]

Kairos—Living in the Now

Some time ago I received a phone call from Warren, a friend from college. He had dropped out of school and returned to his home state of Iowa, where he roomed with a college buddy and delivered pizzas. Because of his heart for teenagers, he was a youth sponsor with his church's youth group. He led Bible studies and helped coordinate activities and retreats.

As much as he enjoyed the teens, Warren felt a real need for friends his age. He said that his phone bill was awful because he had been calling college friends all over the place. I asked if he was finding fellowship with peers, and he told me that, "Except for my roommate, there's nothing. There's no fellowship for people our age. In my church, there's the adults above us and the kids beneath us, and here we are right in the middle."

Warren was in a position where he could pick up where he left off and reenter the college experience. And he did just that; he went back to school to finish up his degree. And I envied him for that.

When we long for a past community, we need to remind ourselves that we need to live in the present, not in the past. I once heard a sermon that said that Christians should reaffirm for themselves the statement, "I am committed to Christ." And the verb tense is very important—I *am* committed to Christ, in the present tense. The speaker said that too many Christians live in the past, thinking of all the great experiences they have had, victories won, achievements accomplished. On the other hand, many Christians wait for the future; they think that they'll really be able to serve God "when I graduate" or "when I get married" or "when I get to the mission field." While we can learn from the past and should plan for the future, we need to *live in the present.*

The singles ministry at my church is named Kairos. *Kairos* is one of the Greek words for time. The other word, *chronos,* is used in the sense of time as a measurement of history, it's the root of our word *chronological.* The sense of *kairos* time is different. *Kairos* is usually used in the Bible to designate a specific moment in time, often with the connotation of a moment of opportunity. For example, at the beginning of Jesus' ministry, he announced, "The time [*kairos*] has come! The kingdom of God is near" (Mk 1:15). That time was a *kairos* moment of time.

In some cases, the NIV translates *kairos* as "opportunity," as in Galatians 6:10, where Paul writes, "Therefore, as we have opportunity [*kairos*], let us do good to all people, especially to those who belong to the family of believers." Similarly, in Ephesians 5:15-16, he writes, "Be very careful, then, how you live—not as unwise but as wise, making the most of every opportunity [*kairos*—other translations say "redeeming the time"] because the days are evil."

But *kairos* moments can be used for evil as well as for good. For example, in Luke 4:13, at the end of the account of the temptation of Jesus, we read that "when the devil had finished all this tempting, he left him until an opportune time *[kairos]*." We need to be on guard that our present opportunities do not become temptations for sin. A proper perspective for the single life is to see every day as a *kairos* moment—an opportunity for either good or evil. Christians are called to do our best to follow Jesus daily.

Maybe we can compare how we live our lives to how we watch movies on our VCRs. Some people like to rewind, to get back to good parts that have already gone past. Others want to fast-forward to parts that haven't happened yet. But movies (and life) are best experienced when we let the tape play—without excessive use of rewind, fast forward, pause or stop.

A Time of Reckoning

A central theme of the Christian experience is death. We look to Jesus' death and resurrection as the events that accomplished our salvation. There is no greater love, Jesus said, than laying down our lives for our friends. Paul writes, "I have been crucified with Christ and I no longer live" (Gal 2:20), and he says that for him "to live is Christ and to die is gain" (Phil 1:21). To take up one's cross is to be sentenced to death row. However, it is rare for us to consider what it would mean to actually physically die for the cause of Christ.

When I was in high school, I went on a summer urban mission project in inner-city Minneapolis. We volunteered in soup kitchens and food pantries, worked with youth in kids' clubs and led neighborhood Bible studies. In preparation, we discussed the physical risks involved: high crime rates, gang territories and extreme poverty. The pastor we worked with lived across the street from a crack house with a ceramic duck on the front lawn. When the duck was near the doorstep, the crack house was closed; when it was placed by the curb, it was open for business.

Since I grew up in comfortable, middle-class suburbia, this was all very new and frightening to me. Our group leaders warned us that in past years some group members had been threatened and robbed. Part of our preparation was to come to grips with the very real risk of physical injury or perhaps even loss of life. Each of us had to come to the point where we could say, "Yes, I'm scared. I don't know what's going to happen to us, but

I am willing to suffer opposition and risk physical harm because I believe in the importance of this ministry in the name of Christ."

That was a time of reckoning. Until then I had never really considered the magnitude of what it meant to be willing to die for the gospel. But that time of reckoning taught me that there was more to the Christian faith than just going to church on Sunday. I began to understand that, ultimately, following Christ means that I am willing to give up my own life if by doing so I may bring others to know him.

Singles also come to a time of reckoning. Almost everybody grows up expecting to marry. From childhood we start envisioning our future mate and dreaming about that future family. We live with the expectation of marriage. Because one plans on having a mate, to not have one implies a sense of loss and incompleteness, leading to feelings of loneliness and failure. But as adulthood continues, we encounter a transition time when we discover that our dreams may have been unrealistic.

"It is not wrong to hope for marriage or to recognize that marriage is a possibility for the future," Gary Collins says, "but it is not healthy to build our lives around events that are uncertain. Instead, individuals, especially Christians, must learn both to prepare for the future and to live fully in the present."[10]

We must recognize that some things in life are more important than whether or not we will ever marry. We must face the fact that marriage may not be a possibility. When I come to this point, I completely hand over my life to God—all my dreams, hopes and desires for a spouse—and tell him that my first priority will be to find my identity in Christ and him alone. This reckoning is a *kairos* moment—a significant moment in time in which I acknowledge that I am called to live my life fully for Christ regardless of my marital status.

I have always liked Paul's metaphor in Romans 12:1 of offering our bodies as "living sacrifices." Many have joked that the problem with living sacrifices is that they keep trying to crawl off the altar. To consciously place the hope for marriage in the hands of God is to make a living sacrifice. I have been deeply impressed with Presbyterian pastor Cliff Bajema's meditation on this passage:

If I tell God that I'll give up eating sweets for a month when sweets are really not something I desire anyway, then I am offering a dead sacrifice. If I tell God I'll do something or yield something to him which is no struggle for me anyway, the sacrifice is not really a sacrifice. It is religious tokenism; it is heavenly-brownie-points accumulation.

But suppose some desire is intensely active in my flesh and has reached the dimension of an addiction. Whether it is food, or a drug, or sex, or a certain person I'm in love with, or a professional objective, or gratifying thoughts of revenge, or soothing emotions of self-pity, or . . . whatever, then for me to say to God "I will yield this addiction to you" is a terribly difficult thing to do. It becomes a *living* sacrifice. Sacrifice is living when it hurts, when it costs me something.[11]

If the desire to marry is overwhelming, if thoughts of marriage dominate our thinking, and if every person of the opposite sex is viewed as a potential marital partner, then the desire for marriage has become idolatrous. It is almost a lust for marriage, not unlike a lust for sex. I once read about a man who complained that single women he met stared at his bare ring finger the way men might stare at a woman's breasts. Much like being seen as a sex object, he felt as if he was being viewed as a "marriage object."

Such desires are unhealthy. They are not only alive, they are alive too much. Cells that are more alive than normal are cancerous. Such unhealthy desires need to be excised, surgically removed, put to death. That is what a living sacrifice is—putting to death the part of us that is alive too much.

"God asks of us a *living* sacrifice," Bajema writes. "He asks us to give over to his control what is alive in us and needs to be redirected to God's glory."[12]

Richard Foster calls this kind of "reckoning"—this living-sacrifice experience—"relinquishment." The way of relinquishment is the movement from "my will be done" to "not my will, but yours." This process involves struggle, because it is difficult to give up those desires and dreams that are so dear to us. But this is just part of the process. Foster says,

Struggle is important because the Prayer of Relinquishment is Christian prayer and not fatalism. We do not resign ourselves to fate. . . . We are not locked into a preset, determinist future. Ours is an open, not a closed universe. We are "co-laborers with God," as the apostle Paul put it—working with God to determine the outcome of events. Therefore our prayer efforts are a genuine give and take, a true dialogue with God—and a true struggle.[13]

The result of such a prayer of relinquishment is that God transforms us through what Foster calls the "crucifixion of the will." This crucifixion results in "death to the self-life. But there is also releasing with hope."[14]

Some singles may fear that such a time of reckoning is akin to taking monastic vows. Not so. A reckoning does not mean that you have condemned yourself to lifetime celibacy, nor does it mean that God will supernaturally zap away all desire for marriage. It only means that you place yourself before God and offer your humble service to him as a single person without an idolatrous desire for marriage. If, having a healthy, nonobsessive view of marriage, you have taken this step, God may very well later present you with the opportunity to marry. Just because we relinquish our dreams and hopes to God does not mean that he goes out of his way to make sure we never get what we want in life. God does not immediately strike dead anybody willing to die for him!

No, reckoning and relinquishment do not mean that we lose all that we have ever hoped for in life. Foster reminds us, "We are dealing with the crucifixion of the will, not the obliteration of the will. Crucifixion always has resurrection tied to it."[15] Death is a central theme in Christian theology only because it prepares the way for the glory of the resurrection. God allows us to continue living after the reckoning point because people who are fully committed to him can be the most productive for the cause of Christ. A person who gives up his or her personal dreams for marriage and family in lieu of service to God can later become a far healthier spouse and parent.

"Relinquishment is not a state at which we arrive suddenly, nor once and for all," one single has written. "It is a slow pilgrimage, and there are many stumblings and bruisings along the way."[16] Such a reckoning is not only for singles. All Christians need to come to the point where they place God as the top priority in their lives, over all other competing allegiances of family, work and other loyalties. Not to their neglect, of course; prioritization of God as Lord of all redirects the believer to properly face the various responsibilities of life.

The late Walter Trobisch wisely wrote:

The art of giving up, of renouncing, is also the secret of happiness in a single person's life. To give up one's self is as important for a single person as it is for one who is married. Those who learn this art will never be lonesome, even if they are single. Those who don't will always be lonesome, even though they are married.[17]

Most people live in tension between the past that can't be recaptured and the future that is not yet realized. We would do well to remember the lesson of those who wanted to follow Jesus but had to do other things first. One man said, "Lord, first let me go and bury my father." Jesus responded, "Let the dead bury their own dead, but you go and proclaim the kingdom of God." Another said, "I will follow you, Lord; but first let me go back and say goodby to my family." To that, Jesus replied, "No one who puts his hand to the plow and looks back is fit for service in the kingdom of God" (Lk 9:59-62).

Ultimately, the reason why singles need to give God their dreams for marriage is the same reason for which Peter left his nets—to follow Jesus. In our times of loneliness, too often singles think, "I will follow you, Lord, but first . . ." But first, let me get married. But first, let me have a spouse I can spend my life with. This is conditional Christianity. We ought not say to God, "Lord, I'll follow you wherever you go and do whatever you ask— but I'm telling you, I could do it better if I was married." Such a grudging spirit is not following Jesus wholeheartedly. Jesus might reply, "I have called you to follow me now, whether or not you ever marry someday. Trust me and follow me. Look to me, not to the dream of a spouse." In Trobisch's words, "God does not like the decisions for a lifetime which we make out of resignation and disappointment. He wants us to live our life this day and to discover all the joyous possibilities of it with confidence and courage."[18]

Beyond Loneliness

It is not enough to try to empty ourselves of our loneliness. Nature abhors a vacuum, and something must replace the emotional space that the loneliness previously filled. Otherwise, our hearts will be like that of the man who had one evil spirit cast out, but because the house was empty, seven more moved in (Mt 12:43-45).

After a time of reckoning and relinquishment, there must also be a time of filling. Reckoning empties the self of desires for marriage which may have been unhealthy. At that point of brokenness and emptiness, loneliness is replaced with identity and sufficiency in Christ. Our identity is transformed from an incomplete, unfulfilled single in search of a mate to a person who is becoming whole and complete in his or her identity as a follower of Christ.

"You are worried that you might end up miserably single? Come to me, all you who are weary and heavily burdened, and I will give you rest.

For my yoke is easy, and my burden is light." He offers single people a far greater joy than that which marriage can provide. He calls them, as he calls married people, to follow him. . . .

Suppose a miserable, lonely single woman met Jesus and poured out her woes. . . . What would Jesus say to her? Would he echo her mother's advice, that she ought to get out and meet some men? Perhaps. Far more certainly, he would invite her—no, call her—to be his disciple now, in her present condition as a single person.[19]

One single found it helpful to remember that "I am complete alone, not a half looking for another half or a melody looking for a harmony. We're all alone, but we're complete as individuals." Our identity is not bound up in our relationships with other people, in a marriage or family or organization. We are complete as individuals, and it is as individuals that we find wholeness and identity in Christ.

Many singles struggle with how to find this fulfillment in Christ. Some do so with mixed motives, seeing Christian commitment only as a means to an end. The subconscious thinking goes, *If I love God enough, maybe he'll give me a spouse.* This is how many Christian singles interpret Psalm 37:4, "Delight yourself in the Lord and he will give you the desires of your heart." We tend to think, "Well, the desire of my heart is to get married. So if I delight myself in the Lord, he will give me someone to marry."

This approach is misguided because it makes our love of God conditional, like being good a few weeks before Christmas so Santa Claus will give us what we want. We have missed the point of this verse. A cause and effect is there, but not the one we think.

Martyred missionary Jim Elliot wrote in 1949 on this verse, "It does not say He will give you what you want. It does say He will give you *the want*. Delight in Christ brings desire for Christ. He gives the heart its desires— that is, He works in us the willing . . . My will becomes His, and I can ask what I will, if I delight myself in Him. Only then can my desire be attained, when it is His desire."[20]

The desires of our hearts can be very selfish and impure. We are often entirely wrongheaded in what we want. So delight in the Lord does not somehow trigger God to answer our indulgent prayers; instead, delight in the Lord transforms the desires of our hearts and shows us what God would desire for us. If we delight ourselves in the Lord, we come to see the pettiness of our earthly desires and how insufficient our limited

dreams are for ultimate fulfillment. God is calling us to find a deeper fullness in him—not by fulfilling our own desires, but discovering his.

The Discipline of Solitude

After college, I was used to having people around all the time and sharing living space with roommates. So it was something of a shock to
start living by myself. Unless I turned on the stereo or TV, it was quiet.
I could spend an entire day by myself without speaking a word to anyone. It was odd to sit at home by myself on a Friday night with nothing to do.

But gradually I came to realize the benefits of living alone. I was no
longer frustrated with the conflicts that naturally come from living with
other people. If there were dishes in the sink, they were *my* dishes. If the
bathroom or bedroom was messy, it was *my* mess.

More significantly, I discovered that I didn't need to go out every weekend and do something social. I could spend a relaxing evening at home on
a Saturday night and read a book. I gradually came to realize that I could be
alone without feeling insecure, awkward or lonely. And rather than experiencing God only through fellowship with the body, I could meet him in the
quietness of an empty apartment. In short, I was discovering solitude.

Solitude can be a misleading term, so we must define what it is and
what it is not. Solitude is not just avoiding other people. It is difficult in
our modern society to escape the hustle and bustle of rush-hour traffic
jams, answering machines, deadlines, committee meetings, itineraries and
schedules. But getting away from it all is not in itself solitude, because
often when we leave behind one form of busyness we simply exchange it
for another. We all know how holidays and vacations can actually be more
draining than the daily grind.

Also, solitude does not mean escaping from the world. The late Henri
Nouwen writes that when most of us think of solitude, we call to mind
pictures of reclusive monks or hermits living in deserts and forests, far
away from the rest of the world. But neither is this, by itself, solitude.

Nouwen makes a critical distinction between *solitude* and *privacy*.
Privacy, he says, is construed as some sort of commodity, a "spiritual property" to which we feel entitled, as when we speak of a "right to privacy."
In this sense, we think of solitude as "a station where we can recharge our
batteries, or as the corner of the boxing ring where our wounds are oiled,

our muscles massaged and our courage restored by fitting slogans." In other words, our privacy-based concept of solitude is nothing more than "a place where we gather new strength to continue the ongoing competition in life."

This concept is very different from the spiritual discipline of solitude. Nouwen says that true solitude is "not a private therapeutic place. Rather, it is the place of conversion, the place where the old self dies and the new self is born, the place where the emergence of the new man and the new woman occurs."[21] Such a solitude is internal; "The solitude that really counts is the solitude of the heart; it is an inner quality or attitude that does not depend on physical isolation."[22]

Solitude accomplishes a transformation of our loneliness. "Jesus calls us from loneliness to solitude," Richard Foster writes. "Loneliness is inner emptiness. Solitude is inner fulfillment."[23] Solitude is not just being alone; it is being alone with God. Because God is transcendent and omnipresent, he is always with us. But we must consciously apprehend his presence before we enter into solitude. Otherwise we are just alone with ourselves and our own thoughts.

What happens to us in solitude? We discover a form of freedom. Dallas Willard, in *The Spirit of the Disciplines,* identifies fifteen spiritual disciplines. He places solitude first in his list because "solitude frees us. . . . Nothing but solitude can allow the development of a freedom from the ingrained behaviors that hinder our integration into God's order."[24]

Furthermore, when we are in solitude, we come to grips with our own humanity and fallenness. Nouwen writes of the early church desert fathers who fled into the wilderness to escape the evils of society, only to discover that through their aloneness, God showed them the depths of their own sins. Nouwen describes his own experience:

In solitude I get rid of my scaffolding: no friends to talk with, no telephone calls to make, no meetings to attend, no music to entertain, no books to distract, just me naked, vulnerable, weak, sinful, deprived, broken—nothing. It is this nothingness that I have to face in my solitude, a nothingness so dreadful that everything in me wants to run to my friends, my work, and my distractions so that I can forget my nothingness and make myself believe that I am worth something.[25]

Foster writes, "If we possess inward solitude we do not fear being alone, for we know that we are not alone."[26] God is with us always, and our being alone does not and cannot change his love and concern for us. The discipline of solitude helps us recognize this fact.

But solitude does not stop there. Solitude actually creates in us a greater appreciation for community, because when we are alone, we recognize our own humanity, our own failings.

In solitude we realize that nothing human is alien to us, that the roots of all conflict, war, injustice, cruelty, hatred, jealousy and envy are deeply anchored in our own heart. In solitude our heart of stone can be turned into a heart of flesh, a rebellious heart into a contrite heart, and a closed heart into a heart that can open itself to all suffering people in a gesture of solidarity.[27]

Such self-understanding creates in us greater compassion for others. Strangers no longer seem as distant, because we perceive them as people who face the struggles of life just as we do. Then we begin to desire relationship and connectedness, for we desire to draw others out of their loneliness and pain and to share with them the fulfillment we have found by encountering God in our solitude. "Thus," Nouwen writes, "in and through solitude we do not move away from people. On the contrary, we move closer to them through compassionate ministry."[28]

We will explore this dynamic further in the next chapter. It is a great paradox of the Christian faith that our loneliness can lead us to solitude, which in turn transforms our aloneness into community. If we develop such a discipline of solitude, we will be better equipped to face the feelings of loneliness that periodically occur. Instead of feeling an inner emptiness, we will feel an inner fulfillment. Being alone will no longer mean that we are social failures, but that we have the opportunity to cultivate our relationship with God. Then we will be whole persons, secure in our identity in the Christ who makes us whole.

Discussion Questions

1. What kind of "little deaths" have you experienced in your life?
2. Do you tend to live in the past, present or future? If your life is a movie, would you prefer to rewind, pause play, fast-forward or stop?
3. Have you ever had a "time of reckoning"? What dreams have you relinquished?
4. Do you agree with the author's interpretation of Psalm 37:4?
5. In what ways have you experienced solitude with God?

7

FROM ALONENESS
TO COMMUNITY

Let him who cannot be alone beware of community.
Let him who is not in community beware of being alone.
DIETRICH BONHOEFFER

Evangelical Christians have traditionally viewed marriage as the cure for aloneness. While few pastors or teachers explicitly say so, such thinking permeates sermons and Christian literature.

For example, a recent end-times novel by two popular evangelical authors describes the experiences of a group of people who are left behind after the Christians mysteriously disappear from the planet.[1] As Rayford, Chloe, Buck and Bruce grapple with the new reality of living in the last days, they come to a knowledge of Christ. At the end of this novel, these four protagonists, who are all single, band together to fight the antichrist. So far the story bodes well for singleness; it pictures singles who can effectively stand against evil in times of trial.

Unfortunately, the sequel negates all this. In the second book, what begins as an exciting premise of life in the end times degenerates into a formulaic romance novel. Two of the main characters, Buck and Chloe, fall in love. In fact, when antichrist figure Nicolae Carpathia offers Buck a seductive career opportunity, what keeps Buck from succumbing is romantic thoughts of Chloe. "Buck fought to keep his mind on Chloe," the narrative says. "Chloe was the object of his attention, and he realized that God had planted these thoughts to help him resist the hypnotic, persuasive power of Nicolae Carpathia."[2]

Christian singles should already find this objectionable. Did God really plant those thoughts of Chloe in Buck's mind? Or was that the result of his own infatuation or lust? The authors seem to suggest that an effective way to flee temptation is to fixate on a romantic love interest (rather than on God). This isn't of much help to singles without a dating partner.

But then we are abruptly introduced to a new character, Amanda, who suddenly becomes Rayford's love interest. And in the last chapter a double wedding takes place for Rayford and Amanda, Buck and Chloe. What follows are several sentimental passages where Rayford finds himself feeling more "whole," now that he has a wife again, and Buck gushes about how Chloe was "the greatest gift God could have granted him" (apart from his salvation, of course).

In stark contrast to these married couples' wedded bliss, the only remaining single character, Bruce, contracts some unknown virus while in Indonesia. As the book ends, he slips into a coma, his hospital is bombed in a terrorist attack and Bruce dies. All of this seems to imply that only married couples could possibly have the fortitude to withstand the tribulations of the last days. Singles might as well roll over and die.[3]

While the authors are no doubt well-intentioned in their exaltation of love and marriage, they fail to recognize how their story marginalizes singles. Though I am reacting to a fictional scenario, my point is that the authors' underlying premise seems to be that Christians really ought to get married. Thus, evangelicalism's obsessive love affair with the nuclear family leaves Christian singles in isolation.

A truly Christian vision of community provides an alternative. We previously made a distinction between loneliness and aloneness. In this chapter we will examine several different levels of aloneness, our need for community and ways singles can develop Christian community.

Personal Aloneness
On the most basic level, aloneness is simply being alone. More and more people are living on their own. In 1970, just under ten million Americans

lived alone, or 7.3 percent of the population. By 1994, that number had risen to over 23.6 million individuals living alone—12 percent, or one in every nine adults. One in four households consists of a person living alone.[4]

Being alone, as we have seen, need not be a negative condition. It can be an opportunity for personal development of our identity with Christ. It is a place where we can cultivate solitude. However, aloneness does have its downside. Most singles feel a tension between the positive and negative aspects of aloneness—independence on the one hand, isolation on the other.[5] One Xer said, "I sometimes feel that if I didn't have a roommate I could die tonight and nobody would notice my body until the landlord came to collect rent."[6]

All people who live alone run this risk, especially the young and the elderly. Many single women take self-defense classes to learn how to protect themselves in case of attack. Entire stores are devoted to security systems and equipment. When I lived by myself in the basement of a split-level house, my mom gave me a carbon-monoxide detector for fear that I would suffocate. I carry a slip of paper in my wallet with a list of names and phone numbers to notify in case of emergency. It would be awful to be in a car accident without anybody knowing of the situation.

Such is the plight of many people who live alone. In the summer of 1995, a killer heat wave swept through Chicago. Hundreds of people died from the heat, most of them senior citizens living in the inner city without air conditioning. Tragically, some of the bodies were not discovered for days or weeks because they lived alone and nobody checked up on them. When it was all over, several dozen bodies could not be identified, and no relatives came forward to claim them. They were anonymously buried in simple wood coffins in a community grave site. That is personal aloneness.

Generational Aloneness

A phenomenon that is now being recognized is *generational aloneness*. More than just physically *being* alone, this is a level at which we *feel* alone. People have felt alone in every age, but the present young adult generation may more acutely feel a sense of being alone in the universe. Janet Bernardi, a Generation X author, describes a friend who felt that she was unable to trust or rely on anyone. A child of divorce, this young woman felt abandoned by her father and ignored by her mother, who left her with a nanny. Her brother repeatedly failed to keep promises to her. Bernardi writes,

My friend cannot rely on her family for support—nor can she rely on her mechanic to be honest, her doctor to prescribe only the tests that are necessary, her friends to help bear her burdens, or strangers to be kind. She feels afraid of being shot, afraid of being held up at the cash machine, afraid of being alone on a date with a man. Like many Xers her age, she is financially independent and lives with roommates. But no one really needs her and she needs no one. This is aloneness.[7]

Generational aloneness is the feeling that I do not matter in the grand scheme of things. It is the grim sense that I could disappear and nobody would notice, let alone care. "Aloneness is being alone and not being able to trust anyone," Bernardi writes. Aloneness does not mean that we are reclusive hermits hiding in the woods, never interacting with other people. Rather, though we are immersed in the very midst of society, we feel as insignificant as one drop of water in a gigantic typhoon. We interact with coworkers and colleagues, but our lives do not really touch each other on a deep personal level. We lack connectedness. Bernardi writes,

While loneliness is a state of emptiness, in aloneness one's life is full of activities but without the aid of family or friends. It encompasses a basic distrust of people and a fear of being hurt. Aloneness is largely about fear. It stems from abandonment or neglect and leads to alienation from friends, family and society. Aloneness is a survival technique and comes across as independence. Aloneness separates this generation from every other.[8]

For some, this feeling of aloneness may be self-inflicted. Or it may be evidence of past hurts. Douglas Coupland defines this phenomenon as the "cult of aloneness": "The need for autonomy at all costs, usually at the expense of long-term relationships. Often brought about by overly high expectations of others."[9] For today's wounded young adults, personal aloneness and generational aloneness team up as a vicious double whammy—a psychological one-two punch.

Societal Individualism and Alienation

Furthermore, our modern society depersonalizes the individual. When I go to the grocery store, I do not know the cashiers. Their only role in my life is to check out my groceries and collect my money. It doesn't matter who they are; all that matters is what they do. Chances are that I will never see this cashier again, even if I come back every week. We may not even make eye contact during our transaction.

In an age where the number of college graduates each year far outnumbers the available entry-level jobs in most fields, multitudes of people clamor for every position. A friend told me of an elementary school that had an opening for a teacher: soon after the job was posted, the office received over six thousand résumés.

The net effect is that the individual is replaceable. I have little significance on the job, because if I quit or am fired, the employers will have no trouble finding a replacement. Bernardi describes her own job situation as typical: "One of my coworkers, who has about the same training and experience as I, was replaced by an eighteen-year-old high school graduate—who can be paid less. Like many people my age, I work at a job where I could be easily replaced. We know that no one really needs us. We could disappear, and nothing would change."[10]

A further symptom is the rise of the temporary worker. One summer I did some temp work because I needed the flexibility to accommodate summer session courses. So I bounced from assignment to assignment, doing word processing at one place and data entry at another, then helping install copier machines at a third. In every place, my coworkers and supervisors were friendly but guarded. I didn't get to know anybody on a personal level, and nobody bothered to really get to know me, because I would be gone in a few days or weeks. It wasn't worth their time to invest in establishing a friendship.

Furthermore, a capitalistic economy tends to work against relationships and connectedness. It is hard to build friendships if we must compete with our colleagues to fight our way up the corporate ladder or just hang on to our present rung.

Bernardi describes this situation as being "like random molecules bumping into other molecules."[11] Similarly, Frank Kirkpatrick calls this model of society the "atomistic" model of community. In such a society, people exist as solitary, isolated individuals, much like atoms or molecules bouncing off each other, competing for resources and position.

As Robert Paul Wolff has put it in summarizing the philosophy of individualistic liberalism, "It is as though society were an enclosed space in which float a number of spherical balloons filled with an expanding gas. Each balloon increases in size until its surface meets the surface of the other balloons; then it stops and adjusts to its surroundings." The balloons, the expanding atoms of a mechanical, contract-based social order, do not feel for each other, they do not live for each other, they do not find their essential nature fulfilled only in communion with each other. As competitors for space and the limited resources necessary for self-advancement, the atoms must always be on their guard against others. . . .

As Erich Fromm . . . has said, "Modern society consists of 'atoms' (if we use the Greek equivalent of 'individual'), little particles estranged from each other but held together by selfish interests and by the necessity to make use of each other."[12]

The Need for Community

The NBC show *Friends* was the most popular new sitcom of the 1994-95 TV season. It received eight Emmy nominations. It ranked as the number six show of the season and was the highest-rated new comedy of the year for adults aged eighteen to forty-nine and for homes.

Why was *Friends* so successful? It's the story of six single young adults in their twenties experiencing life in New York City. These three men and three women hang out in a coffeehouse together, share emotional traumas and approve or disapprove of each other's dates. The hit theme song, "I'll Be There for You," by the Rembrandts, captures the dreams of a generation—the ideal of finding a community of close friends who are always there for each other, no matter what.

On the NBC *Friends* World Wide Web site on the Internet, executive producers Kevin Bright, Marta Kauffman and David Crane comment, "*Friends* is a show about love, sex, careers and a time in life when everything is possible. It's about searching for commitment and security—and a fear of commitment and security. And, most of all, *Friends* is a show about friendship—because when a person is young and single in the city, friends and family are synonymous."

Cast member David Schwimmer remarked that one of the reasons for the show's popularity was that "it is a fantasy for a lot of people, having a group of friends who replace the family."[13]

While *Friends* may leave much to be desired in terms of ethics and morality, it does depict something that Christian singles yearn for. Connectedness. Community. A place to belong. People to rely on. It is no accident that many singles make a habit of getting together every

Thursday night to watch *Friends,* perhaps hoping that in their own group friendships will grow and develop into community.

The antidote for aloneness and alienation is community. While it is good for us to develop solitude, we are not meant to stay alone all the time. We are social beings, designed to live in relationship with others. While some may genuinely prefer to live solitary, isolated lives, most of us yearn to belong to a group and have a place where we are acknowledged and needed. Oswald Sanders writes, "People were created with a twofold need—fellowship with God and companionship with other human beings."[14] Fellowship with God is the solution for loneliness. Companionship with fellow Christians is the cure for aloneness.

Our identity with Christ, though personal and individual, is also corporate and communal. The discipline of solitude should not isolate us—solitude should move us toward community. Solitude actually helps us appreciate people more. Solitude and community are two parallel disciplines, two sides of the same coin, which need to be held in balance.

Someone has compared this paradox to appreciating a mountain. In order to truly grasp the magnitude of the mountain, one does not poke around on it and examine a small area up close. One needs to withdraw several miles until it is possible to see the whole mountain. Only then we can appreciate its size. And after we have seen the mountain from a distance, we will have a higher appreciation for the view from the top.

Similarly, being in solitude generates in us a desire to be in community. In order to truly appreciate fellowship and community, we need to spend time by ourselves. Henri Nouwen writes, "Solitude not only deepens our affection for others but also is the place where real community becomes possible."[15]

In our society, this yearning for connectedness is seen in the boom in personal ads and dating services. Of course, such methods of meeting people tend to be very artificial. Anyone who has gone on a blind date can testify that the expectation of the set-up creates its own awkwardness. "The fact that we tend to make meeting people its own individual activity may actually be the reason we have so little success doing it," Dave said. So where can we find genuine community?

The Church as First Family

Paul was no stranger to the problems of alienation and aloneness. When writing to the Ephesians, he said, "Remember that at that time you were separate from Christ, excluded from citizenship in Israel and foreigners to the covenants of the promise, without hope and without God in the world" (Eph 2:12). Some of us can relate to this situation. We know what it feels like to be excluded, to feel separated from others—to be the last person chosen for the kickball team or to sit at an empty lunchroom table. We know what it's like to be lost and confused, both lonely and alone.

But God has good news for the single person who feels alone and alienated: "But now in Christ Jesus you who once were far away have been brought near through the blood of Christ" (Eph 2:13). We were once far away—outcasts, outsiders, out of the loop—but God has brought us right into the midst of his community. Through Christ we are "no longer foreigners and aliens, but fellow citizens with God's people and members of God's household" (Eph 2:19). In love he adopted us to be his children (Eph 1:5). We were orphaned, without a family to call our own. But God adopted us! God chose us—the ones nobody else wanted to take in. He accepted us and made us his children.

The metaphor of adoption is significant. Most parents love a biological child because it is their own flesh and blood. They feel an innate kindredness to those who are their own. But adoptive parents *choose* to love someone who is not theirs. They are under no obligation to care for the adopted child, but they bring the child into their home because of intentional, extravagant love. And such is the love God has for us. He has adopted us and chosen to take us into his household.

The household imagery is also important. Once we come to Christ, we cannot pretend that we are alone in the world. God has brought us into his community—a community of those who share salvation and profess faith in Christ. Singles often try to find community and connectedness by finding someone to marry and start a family with. But our primary means for connectedness is not the biological or marital family. Rodney Clapp has written that we need to recover the sense of the church as "first family," saying that for the Christian, the family is not the primary source of community. Instead,

> the church is God's most important institution on earth. The church is the social agent that most significantly shapes and forms the character of Christians. The church is the primary vehicle of God's grace and salvation for a waiting, desperate world.[16]

While we may come to Christ as individuals, we do not remain solitary salvation pilgrims or individual Lone Ranger Christians. "Jesus does not merely call individuals qua individuals, who will separately and simply await death and the bodiless joys of heaven. Instead, he forms a community on earth."[17] Being a Christian is not an individual journey; it is a group effort lived in community. Cyprian wrote in the third century, "He cannot have God for his father who has not the Church for his mother."[18]

Of course, it is possible for singles to find friendships and interaction with others through any number of non-Christian venues, including health clubs, bowling leagues, political parties, fraternal lodges and business associations. Such organizations can certainly be beneficial for social interaction. However, the *primary* place for Christian singles to find fulfilling relationships and identification is in the Christian community.

> The New Testament indicates that the primary community for the Christian is to be the believing community, the church. And the primary bond is the covenant with God in Christ, and by extension with the covenant community. While this is to be true for all Christians regardless of marital status, the single Christian often experiences this primary bonding in a more vibrant way. For the single Christian the church can become not only ideally and theoretically but also quite practically the source of highest fellowship and the focal point for the development of one's closest relationships. Single believers readily look to their congregation to be "family" in the primary sense and discover within the church membership their deepest friends.[19]

Some may object and say, "Can't I be a Christian without joining the church?" The answer is, "Yes, it is a possibility, but it would resemble the student who desires to learn but has no desire for school. It would be like the professional athlete who loves his sport, but has no desire to practice or train."[20] As many have observed, a campfire burns only when all the wood and coals are placed together. An ember taken away, standing on its own, soon dies out.

A healthy, growing Christian life requires being part of Christian community. "Essential to our growth in grace is a community life where there is loving, nurturing accountability. Christlikeness is not merely the work of the individual; rather, it grows out of the matrix of a loving fellowship. We are the body of Christ together, called to watch over one another in love."[21]

Some Christian groups focus on the nuclear family, claiming that the fundamental building block of a godly civilization is the individual family unit. This is not true. "In subordinating the natural family to the kingdom, Jesus was apparently indicating that it, too, stands in need of redemption."[22] Our society is rife with examples testifying to the pain that families inflict on their members. Like all human institutions, the biological family has been tainted with sin and requires transformation and reconciliation with God. There is nothing inherently noble or virtuous about the nuclear family.

Far more instrumental in accomplishing God's purposes on earth is the united community of the church. "With the coming of the kingdom—a kingdom that manifests itself physically as well as spiritually, socially as well as individually, and in the present as well as in the future—Jesus creates a new family. It is the first family, a family of his followers that now demands primary allegiance. In fact, it demands allegiance even over the old first family, the biological family."[23]

For singles who yearn for a sense of belonging to a spouse and family, God reminds us that we are part of a family far more significant and enduring than the biological family. In one sense we are already married—as the bride of Christ.

Singles in the Church

The next question is, "Is there a place for singles in today's churches?" Christian singles well know that the church has not done a very good job of including singles as part of its community. Protestants have inherited the Reformation emphasis on marriage and family. The evangelical church has traditionally been a place for the family, especially couples with children. Lyle Schaller, a consultant for church ministries, describes local churches as having many "doors" which newcomers can walk through to become involved in the church. The door for couples and families may be wide open, but the door for singles may seem shut tight, with a "hand-lettered sign tacked to the door which declares Temporarily Closed: Come Back When You're Married and Have Two Children."[24]

Many singles feel alone in their churches. As in the high-school lunchroom, the problem now is that a single enters the sanctuary and has no one to sit with. "I felt terribly left out at one church that was a young-marrieds church," a single man said. "I went there for several years and I was always the token single guy."

Gary Collins writes,

Contacts in singles bars or night spots can be fleeting and destructive, so some people turn to the church. Many find, however, that they are unwelcome or at best tolerated by church members who don't understand, don't know how to relate to singles, and sometimes blatantly reject unmarried people, especially if they are divorced. . . .

Something is wrong with a church that sees single adults as misfits, has no place in the body for unmarried people, lacks programs to meet the needs of singles and shows no understanding (or desire to understand) their struggles (especially if the single person is divorced).[25]

Sometimes pastors are resistant to the idea of a singles ministry. Singles often rank low on their list of priorities. Church staff members may reason, "Well, we don't have many singles in our church, so we shouldn't focus on them. Our church has more people who are married with children, so we have to use our resources to provide for their needs."

But the question is one of cause and effect. Are the low numbers of singles justification for not having a singles ministry? Or is the fact that no singles ministry exists the reason why few singles are in the church?

Many churches have effective singles ministries, with singles groups where single adults feel comfortable and welcome without being stereotyped or pigeonholed. Churches with a large enough single population are able to diversify their ministries to meet the needs of singles in different age groups. A twenty-two-year-old recent college graduate has different concerns and issues than a forty-five-year-old divorcee. One prominent megachurch has a singles fellowship group for singles in their twenties, another for those in their thirties, and yet another for those in their forties and up. Other churches make no such distinction and offer different classes based on topic, which all singles are free to choose from.

But what if your church has no singles group? Start one!

The idea for the singles group at my church, Blanchard Road Alliance Church in Wheaton, Illinois, started in the fall of 1993, with three Wheaton College Graduate School students, Karyn, John and Eric. They tried attending several Sunday-school classes but didn't find a place where they felt they fit in. The church had a college group and a young marrieds group but nothing specifically for singles.

Karyn remembers that the three of them met for lunch one day and just jokingly talked about starting a class for single adults. They went home for Christmas, and when they came back, they found that they had all been thinking about the idea.

"We thought that God might be leading us in the direction of leading a singles ministry," Karyn said. They began to formulate ideas of what the group would look like and drew up a mission statement. Then they met with the pastoral staff, who told them, "This sounds great! We want you guys to go for it!"

So in the spring of 1994, Kairos was launched as an opportunity for singles aged twenty-two to thirty-five to grow in their relationship with Christ. Eric played guitar and led worship, and Karyn and John taught. The emphasis was on building community, using small groups and outside activities to develop relationships among the members of the group. A core group of about ten regular attenders developed in the first few weeks. It gradually continued to grow. Within a year, several dozen people were active members of Kairos.

Singles Community Dynamics

Singles groups do not just automatically happen, of course. They require people with initiative and vision to facilitate the building of the group. Kairos now has a leadership team that is responsible for the activities of the group, from the teaching during our Sunday morning class to birthday parties to small-group Bible studies and special activities. Our group is completely lay-led, which helps us have a sense of ownership of the group. To provide clear direction, we have crafted a vision statement that identifies Kairos as "a Christian community of single adults committed to encouraging one another to lead obedient, fulfilling lives as followers of Jesus Christ."[26]

But every singles community will encounter challenges. One problem is transience. Studies show that "the average singles group in America turns over its population from 40 to 60 percent every six months."[27] The nature of singles groups is that members come and go: they move, marry or go elsewhere to have their needs met. The lack of permanence can prevent people from getting deeply involved.

Our group changes drastically from week to week. One week forty people may be in attendance. The next week forty may be there again, but half may be newcomers. We accept it as a reality of life. "Singles groups are hard because people come and go and come and go," said Jen, a member of the

Kairos leadership team. "But you get to meet a lot of people that way."

Part of this transience is that some singles hop from church to church in order to meet more people of the opposite sex. This is especially true in communities where a number of churches have growing singles ministries. It is not uncommon for singles to participate in activities in two or more churches, often for the sole purpose of maximizing their contacts with potential mates.

"A lot of sharks swim around singles groups, just looking for someone to date," one single said. "Every woman who comes in just gets ogled." Some unhealthy singles groups are Christian dating services at best and meat markets at worst. Singles ministries need to be aware that sexual predators may join their group in order to target the unsuspecting and vulnerable.

"A singles group suffers when it becomes exclusively a launching pad for escape from singleness," Stafford writes. "Sometimes such groups seem to underline a non-Christian message: that sex is the end-all and be-all of life. Thus single people meet in the church instead of the singles bar, but with the same ultimate response—to escape the hell of celibacy."[28]

A healthy singles community requires a healthy perspective. Teaching in singles ministries should emphasize that the primary purpose of the group is not to find a mate, but to exemplify Christian community by building one another up as followers of Jesus. While it may be a natural starting point to join a group in order to make friends and meet people, spouse hunting is not the primary purpose for the group's existence.

Many singles feel that a certain stigma is attached to "singles groups." One may feel embarrassed to say, "I'm going to the singles group," as if this means, "I'm going to the recovery group for dysfunctional people." A common perception may be that all the people who can't get a spouse go to the singles group to find one. In Kairos, we have tried to eliminate some of this stigma by referring to ourselves as a singles class, singles ministry or singles community.

Furthermore, the gathering together of people is no guarantee of connectedness. It takes time to build trust, to become vulnerable, to share experiences and build community. Connectedness between singles in a singles group develops gradually.

Community means that people come together and hold certain things in common. True Christian community has these three components: a common commitment, common vision and common life.[29]

1. Common commitment: Accountability. A healthy singles community is one in which the members of the group develop close-knit relationships in order to help each other live the Christian life. Members of the group will share their struggles with trusted friends, who will pray for one another in times of need. Singles with a common commitment to Christ will help each other discover and use their gifts.

I saw this kind of caring and concern for one another's well-being one Monday night during our small-group Bible study. For a number of reasons, we were missing a bunch of our regular attenders that night. Rex had just started radiation treatment for a brain tumor and was at home resting. Lindsey called to tell us that she had gotten into a car accident over the weekend and needed to take care of alternative transportation arrangements. Others were sick or studying. Lisa, who was there, needed to leave early in order to move some furniture.

A few of the guys in the group volunteered to help Lisa move her furniture. So we decided to forego the Bible study; Hans and Tim left to help Lisa move, and the rest of us stayed and prayed for those who weren't there. Then when the furniture movers returned, we decided to pile into cars and drive to our missing members' homes to cheer them up. We went to Lindsey's house and serenaded her with "You Are My Sunshine." Then we went to Rex's place and checked in with him to see how his treatment was going. And then we went to see Ryan, who hadn't been attending for a few weeks and was in the midst of studying for grad school midterms. Though he was surprised to see us, he welcomed us in and we played ping-pong and caught up with how he was doing.

The next week Lindsey and Ryan both thanked our group for the visits, saying that we had made their day and that it really meant a lot to them. I was very glad to see how committed the group members were to one another, that they genuinely cared for each other during tough times and missed those who were gone. And it was neat to see our group be so flexible that when our members couldn't make it to small group, we took the small group to them!

2. Common vision: Partnership in ministry. A healthy singles community will also have a shared purpose beyond the group itself. They will gather together not only for their own sake but also to accomplish purposeful ministry goals together. Part of our vision statement reads, "With Jesus' servant leadership as our model, we encourage one another to serve God in kingdom-strategic ways, using our spiritual gifts to impact the lives of other people in our church, our community and our world."

For example, Amy, who is on Kairos's leadership team, also serves on the church missions committee. During our annual missions festival the church hosts a dinner where everybody can hear more about what God is doing worldwide. Amy recruited a group of Kairos members to help prepare for the banquet the night before, by setting up tables and decorating the room.

Cheryl's Thursday night Bible study spent several weeks doing volunteer work. They moved hundreds of chairs around the church sanctuary and vacuumed; they cleaned the houses of people recovering from surgery and baked cookies for them; they helped a first-grade teacher decorate her classroom and wash the windows.

Other service activities include volunteering with homeless shelters and serving at soup kitchens. Many of our singles teach Sunday school or Vacation Bible School, lead children's church and assist with Pioneer Clubs. Often a whole bunch of us will help somebody move and then sit on the boxes and have pizza.

3. Common life: Fellowship. A healthy singles community will be characterized by people who enjoy getting together and sharing in each other's lives. This may be the most visible aspect of the singles community. Besides church on Sunday, Kairos members get together for weekly Bible studies, monthly prayer and praise sessions, camping trips and retreats, surprise birthday parties, seasonal holiday celebrations and even spontaneous slumber parties. Weaving such a tapestry of shared experiences solidifies the bonds within the group.

The act of eating together often helps build relationships. Janet Bernardi has written about "the spirituality of dinner together." She says,

> We wanted desperately to be part of some community of people we could trust. So we created this community by cooking dinner together.
>
> We cooked together often, and found a spirituality in it that we couldn't find in church or in any therapy session. What we did was create a family, a community—something larger than ourselves, but not so large that our individual actions did not have an effect. We sought healing of our broken spirits in the community of others, and we found it.[30]

In my first semester of graduate school, a group of first-year grad students met together for dinner every Sunday night, rotating among our apartments.

Sometimes the host provided the meals; other times we all contributed to a potluck. After church every Sunday, people from Kairos share a meal together, whether meeting in somebody's apartment for brunch or going out to eat. Our Monday night Bible study group has dinner together every week before the study. Some singles groups have "Dinners of Eight," where eight singles get together in someone's home for dinner and fellowship.

The act of eating is especially conducive to building community. It is no coincidence that couples on dates don't just go out to do something; they usually plan on dinner together. Having a meal together signifies an intentional act of building relationship.

Theologian Robert Webber has commented about the significance of eating in the Christian experience. The first act of disobedience was one of eating fruit in the Garden, in which Adam and Eve built a relationship with the serpent and broke one with God. The Jewish community celebrated the acts of God at feasts and festivals such as the Passover and Sabbath meals. Jesus instituted the Lord's Supper and invites us to partake of the bread and the wine. And when the kingdom of God comes in its full glory, we will share the wedding feast of the Lamb.

For Christians, it seems as if wherever two or more are gathered in his name, there is food in their midst. Eating together is sacramental. Food facilitates fellowship.

Educating the Church

Jim told me about a progressive dinner at his church. The cost was advertised as "$8 per couple." The event was not intended to be a couples-only activity; singles were certainly welcome. But the language the church used seemed to exclude singles from participating. Jim wondered, *Couldn't they just as easily have said that the cost would be "$4 per person"?*

As the single adult population grows and those numbers are reflected in church congregations, churches will need to become more sensitive to the way they treat singles. Since churches tend to be places for families with children, sermons are often about marriage or parenting. It's fine to listen to a message that is meant for others in the church and not for you—once in a while. But not every week!

Perhaps churches need sensitivity training in regard to singles, much as they would for other marginalized groups. Just as churches have begun to recognize the need for gender-inclusive language, they need to use language that is inclusive of singles. Churches need to be careful not to have Sunday-school classes named "Pairs and Spares," which demeans singles by implying that they are nonessential spare parts. Form letters should not invite people to "bring your spouse" to church activities; invite folks to bring a spouse or friend.

At a concert of prayer at my church, we spent one block of time praying for the leaders of the church. Many stood and prayed for the ministerial staff and their families, and for the leaders of various ministries in the church. A recurring theme I heard was that people prayed for these leaders to have good family lives, strong marriages and healthy children. Of course, we should pray for these concerns. But what struck me was the presupposition that all the leaders were married with kids. What about leaders who were single? Were they worthy of the church's prayers?

What I wanted to do (but didn't) was to stand and voice a prayer something like this: "Lord, thank you for raising up leaders for the singles group here. I pray for the leadership team and the small group leaders and all the others who serve in Kairos. Help them implement their vision for single adult ministry, so that singles who come to this church can know that they are welcome here, that this is not just a church for married people, but that singles have a place here as well."

On the other hand, our church tries to use language and examples that are inclusive of singles. I remember a lesson about relationships where the pastor said that our primary relationship is with God, followed by relationships with "our friends, roommates and family." That struck me because most pastors would have said something along the lines of "your spouse, family and friends." Including "roommates" helps singles feel as if they are not marginal members of the audience, but a direct priority.

Also, singles communities themselves need to be sensitive to their own terminology. We have tried to discourage any reference to marriage as "graduating" from the group. Graduation implies a completion of an incomplete state of being, which is an incorrect perception of the single life. We prefer to say that people are "transitioning" from singleness to marriage, exchanging one gift for another one of equal value.

Perhaps churches even need to intentionally and verbally make a point of including and welcoming singles from the pulpit. Pastor David Johnson of the Church of the Open Door in Minneapolis discovered that nearly half of the population of his church was single—either never-married, divorced or widowed. In a sermon, Johnson said, "This may sound a little corny, but we've never done this before. To the 48 percent of the population at Church of the Open Door, those single adults among us, I say, 'Hi! Hi! We recognize your presence! We're glad you're here!'"[31]

Such a public statement not only affirms single adults in the church, it also reminds the married population that the church is more than a place for couples with children. The church is for all who follow Jesus, single or married.

Singles and Families Together

Churches are often guilty of fragmenting their membership into disparate groups that rarely interact. There may be great youth groups, but the teens may feel most of the adults in the church are not interested in them. There are classes exclusively for young couples; parents have parenting classes; empty nesters have their own group. And singles, too, are segmented off into their own little world. Singles may have an effective singles community among themselves, but they may not know anybody else in the church. When this is the case, initiative needs to be taken from both sides.

We need to recover the concept of the interrelatedness of the body of Christ. Just as individual Christians need to be a part of the community, so too do singles need interaction with married couples and families. While it is true that singles groups need a certain degree of autonomy in order to build a healthy community, a time should come where singles will interact with the rest of the church body as a whole. We have tried to move our group toward being part of the larger community of Blanchard Road as a whole and not just our own isolated little island.

Rodney Clapp has written that whereas singles have the missionary advantage of mobility, families have the missionary advantage of hospitality.[32] These complementary situations can help provide for each other's needs. A single may feel rootless and miss the interaction with a family. A family may find it difficult to provide all the nurture and guidance required in the task of parenting. A solution to both needs can be for a single to build a relationship with a family. The single can come alongside the parents and help with child care. The family can embrace the single and provide a secondary home.

The New York Times ran an article about a new concept: the "para-parent." It described single mothers who had difficulty juggling the needs of working and parenting.

A growing number of adults are coming to view children as a collective commitment that is more than biological in its impulse. Child care experts are just now beginning to give proper recognition to these unformalized, often serendipitous "para-parenting" arrangements that bind children and single adults. . . . For their part, biological parents say they are seeking stronger support systems for their children. And often it is the children who are initiating these relationships.[33]

The concept of the para-parent is not really new. Aunts, uncles and grandparents have played such a role throughout history. In some communities neighbors still look out for one another's children. But modern realities are making both of these situations rare. Extended family often do not live nearby, and neighborhoods lack connectedness.

The church is the ideal institution for the difficult task of parenting. Instead of parents attempting the job alone, children can be parented with the help of the entire Christian community, young and old, single and married. At my church, members of the singles group serve as "pals" to the youth in Pioneer Clubs. They serve as big brothers or big sisters, providing positive Christian role models for the children. Singles and marrieds work together as Sunday-school teachers and youth sponsors to help children follow Christ.

John Stott said, "Although I have no children of my own, I have hundreds of adopted nephews and nieces all over the world, who call me 'Uncle John.' I cherish these affectionate relationships; they greatly lessen, even if they do not altogether deaden, occasional pangs of loneliness."[34]

In some cases, singles and families can "adopt" each other, in the context of the larger family of the church. Singles may virtually become members of the family. One woman has formed such a close relationship with a family that she has taken the four children along on her own personal vacations, to provide them with valuable experiences as well as to give the parents a break from the parenting responsibility.

Singles can find connectedness and become part of something larger than themselves through interaction with singles groups and with families in the church. A Sunday-school class or small-group Bible study can become a parafamily where singles can discover relationships as significant as those of biological families.[35]

We hope that Kairos can provide a place where people in our church can experience community in ways that other aspects of the church cannot give. In 1995 an engaged couple, Matt and Char, came to our church. They didn't feel comfortable in the classes for couples and instead started attending Kairos. They developed friendships and became active members of our community, and when they married in July 1996 members of our group helped with their wedding by putting together the decorations and providing other practical help, even making the wedding cake.

Since getting married, Matt and Char have continued to participate in Kairos events, though they also attend the young couples' class. They tell us that they appreciate Kairos as a place where they experience community and positive, loving relationships. The fact that they want to continue to be a part of our group after their marriage demonstrates that our vision for community is larger than just a place for singles to pair up and get married. We think it speaks well of us that people aren't there just to find a spouse and then disappear—rather, the community and relationships we embody are so attractive that even those who do marry don't want to leave!

Interestingly enough, in the first family of the church, it is still true that blood is thicker than water. "For those who follow Jesus, the critical blood, the blood that most significantly determines their identity and character, is not the blood of the biological family. It is the blood of the Lamb."[36]

Discussion Questions

1. When have you felt most alone?
2. What do you do when you want to be with people?
3. What experiences have you had with singles groups? Have they been positive or negative?
4. What role models do you have as a single? Is there someone for whom you could act as an encourager? Is there an older Christian you could ask to mentor you?
5. How have you seen singles and families interacting in complementary ways? Is there a family nearby with whom you could explore a closer relationship?

8

....

RETHINKING ROMANCE

*Why would people get married if they did not have
desire and love for each other? Indeed, that is just why God
has given this eager desire to bride and bridegroom,
for otherwise everybody would flee from marriage and avoid it.*
MARTIN LUTHER

We have seen how singles are called to find personal identity in
relationship with God and community in the body of Christ. But what
about the strong desire for a significant other? And how about issues of
sexual temptation—is there hope for the single adult who wants to remain
sexually pure?

Here we shall examine the troublesome issues of romance, dating and
sex. Countless books have been written about the how-to's of these sub-
jects. But beyond trite advice on "finding the right one," we want to
develop an approach to *thinking* about these issues. We shall see that
our view of romance has often been flawed—and that, for those who
pursue dating, there is hope for healthy models of relationships.

From Cinderella to Pocahontas
Most American children grow up on Disney's animated classics. In the
past, Disney has been criticized for presenting its female protagonists as
helpless and in need of a man to save them. This has changed slightly in

the "new Golden age" of Disney animation, with stronger heroines such as Ariel in *The Little Mermaid,* Belle in *Beauty and the Beast* and Jasmine in *Aladdin.* However, these Disney movies still often share a common plot line: A young woman is supposed to marry someone she does not love. Defying parental will, she proclaims that she will not marry unless she is in love with that person. The heroine sings some version of "Someday My Prince Will Come" and then meets her Prince Charming. The hero and heroine overcome all obstacles, profess their true love for each other and live happily ever after. Granted, some movies (such as *Bambi* or *Dumbo*) lack a romantic love theme, but even a canine Lady and a Tramp can find wedded bliss.

This has been the classic formula for generations of Disney films. But how would these movies look without such an ending? What if Cinderella had not lost the glass slipper and Prince Charming had never found her again? Or what if Ariel's father had declared that mermaids simply could not marry humans because of biological incompatibility? Or what if Belle's profession of love for the Beast had come a minute too late and he had died, never to be transformed into her beloved prince?

Think of the plot of *Aladdin.* Suppose our hero had defeated the evil Jafar, but Jasmine's sultan father still decreed that a law was a law and Jasmine still must marry a prince. Would that have been an acceptable ending to the movie? Many moviegoers would have probably left the theater feeling unsatisfied, perhaps even cheated out of the "right" ending. As my friend Gavin wryly observed, "Aladdin would be a loser if he didn't get the girl!"

So runs the Disney/American myth of "happily ever after." It is not enough for good to triumph over evil. Our popular culture reinforces the belief that in order to have a happy ending, the prince and princess must be united in blissful matrimony. To have a complete, fulfilled life, we must find our own real-world counterpart with whom we can share a storybook love. (In the case of *The Lion King,* an additional subtle message might be that in order to participate in the "circle of life," one must not only marry but produce offspring as well.) Western fairy tales, like *Snow White* and *Cinderella,* always have a romantic ending.

However, this "happily ever after" ending is not always the case in stories from other parts of the world. For example, the original Arabian Aladdin story had no princess and no romantic plot line. Apparently the

Disney writers decided that a romanceless fairy tale just wouldn't fly for American audiences. And Hans Christian Andersen ended the original version of his story with the little mermaid's tragic death.

However, one of the newest additions to the Disney legacy seems to defy convention. The 1995 release *Pocahontas* was hailed as the first Disney animated movie that could be considered a serious adult romance. In this movie, true love cannot overcome the realities of life. At the end of the movie, the leading lady doesn't ride off into the sunset with the main man. John Smith and Pocahontas go their separate ways, never to meet again. For the first time, perhaps, "happily ever after" doesn't happen.

Unlike its predecessors, *Pocahontas* is not based on a fairy tale, and perhaps the script writers didn't want to alter history too much. But it raises some interesting questions: Can the story end this way? Can there be a happy ending if the hero and heroine can't be together forever?

Perhaps we can take a cue from *Pocahontas*. Maybe this movie is suggesting to us the possibility of a nonmarried "happily ever after."

The Myth of Romantic Love

Why did popular songs always focus on romantic love? Why this preoccupation with first meetings, sad partings, honeyed kisses, heartbreak, when life was also full of children's births and trips to the shore and longtime jokes with friends? . . . It struck Maggie as disproportionate. Misleading, in fact.[1]

In Western society, romantic love is the ultimate of all ideals. Love overrides reason, logic, good judgment and outside counsel and becomes the final authority for decision-making. How many times has a son or daughter announced to the parents that he or she has fallen in love and, against better judgment and legitimate concerns, intends to marry? All the parents can do is say, "Well, if they really love each other . . ." and hope for the best.

Such sentiments make for popular movies, but they are no guarantee of healthy relationships or enduring marriages. At the heart of this view is the idea that love is an irresistible force, like gravity. Falling in love is like falling off a cliff. If you fall in love, nothing can be done about it. "Inherent to the ethos of romantic love is the notion that it is 'natural' and universally inevitable."[2] Therefore, when Cupid shoots you with his arrow, you're doomed. You have no choice in the matter. In this scenario, love is best when it is accidental and unintended. For example:

"Daniel, I knew you before you knew Karla. Did you ever think then that love was never going to happen to you?"

"Pretty much."

"And when it did happen, how did you feel?"

"Happy. And then I got afraid that it would vanish as quickly as it came. That it was accidental—that I didn't deserve it. It's like this very, very nice car crash that never ends."[3]

In the myth of romantic love, love is an accident, like a car wreck. Or perhaps some divine or cosmic forces are at work behind the scenes, orchestrating events that only *seem* accidental. In either case, lovers are held in the grip of something larger than themselves and beyond their control.

Such a view of love is flawed because instead of having the freedom to choose and make responsible decisions with our lives, we become mere victims of circumstance. People become less than human and instead more like animals in heat who respond only to their hormonal drives. Animals have little control over such urges. On the other hand, humans, created in the image of God, have the ability to choose our own actions and make rational decisions. "We need to call into question the romantic view of love as something 'bigger than both of us' which all of a sudden irrationally reveals to two people that they are 'made for each other,' and irresistibly pushes them toward marriage."[4]

Another key problem with "happily ever after" is that it is vague and ambiguous. What do Snow White and Prince Charming do after they've been riding off into the sunset for five or ten years? A refinanced mortgage, three kids, dirty diapers and credit card bills? We will never know, because the movie ends before it gets that far. "The marrow of the fairytale is never about actually living happily ever after; romantic love cannot even provide us with a description of 'ever after.' It is all about a goal, a goal that can never be achieved but is by definition best dreamed about and pined after."[5] The illusion never connects with reality. "Nothing in the bridal magazines hinted at any form of human existence following the wedding."[6]

We must also recognize that the concept of romantic love is a relatively late development in history. One scholar writes, "The idea of romantic love itself should be recognized as a late, rare, and morally dubious product of Western society, which in many cases does more to destroy marriages than to preserve them."[7] Clapp agrees:

It is only since the Middle Ages that romantic love has been prized as an ideal, the *sine qua non* for marriage and the fully vital human life. Marriage in history has more typically been arranged between families than chosen merely by a man and woman "in love." In fact, in most of Western history the sweeping intensity, confusion and absorption of what we have come to know as romantic love was considered a misfortune.[8]

For example, while modern-day readers might see Romeo and Juliet as the epitome of romantic love stories, we ought to remember that Shakespeare classified the play not as a romance but as a tragedy. He titled it *The Tragedy of Romeo and Juliet*. The story does not glorify the wonder of romantic love. Instead it depicts its dangers. Two starry-eyed kids fall in love and kill themselves because of it. The conclusion of the matter is, "For never was a story of more woe/than this of Juliet and her Romeo." This is no romantic fairy tale of "happily ever after." Shakespeare was not depicting the beauty of romantic love but rather the emotional dangers of being in love too much. *Romeo and Juliet* shows how romantic love, when taken to an extreme, can cause destruction and tragedy.

The Bible offers several stories that illustrate the dangers of romantic love. Judges 16:4 says that Samson "fell in love" with Delilah. Delilah then manipulates Samson's profession of love against him in order to gain the secret of his strength: "How can you say, 'I love you' when you won't confide in me?" (Judg 16:15). Samson gives away his secret, and Delilah immediately betrays him to the Philistines. His hair shaved and his strength gone, Samson is captured by the Philistines, and his eyes are gouged out. Romantic feelings led to a hero's downfall. Samson, quite literally, was blinded by love.

King David, compelled by his emotions and hormones, is drawn to the beautiful Bathsheba (2 Sam 11). We can almost hear his own mental self-justifications, sounding as if spoken today: "I couldn't help it. I got caught up in the emotion of the moment. It felt so right. What else could I do?"

Of course, the story ends in tragedy. David and Bathsheba's adultery produces a child. To cover up the sin, David arranges for Bathsheba's husband to be killed. David is rebuked by the prophet Nathan, and as punishment for their sin, David and Bathsheba's child dies a week after birth.

The very next chapter in 2 Samuel tells the story of David's son Amnon, who was a chip off the old block. Amnon, like his father, fell prey to the power of illicit "love." Second Samuel 13:1 reads, "Amnon son of David fell in love with Tamar, the beautiful sister of Absalom son of David." Amnon pretends to be ill so that his half-sister Tamar will bring food to him. Then he lures her over to the bed and rapes her. "Then Amnon hated her with intense hatred. In fact, he hated her more than he had loved her. Amnon said to her, "Get up and get out!" (2 Sam 13:11-15).

Weeping and disgraced, Tamar goes away to live in her brother Absalom's house, "a desolate woman." Hating Amnon for disgracing his sister, Absalom plots and carries out Amnon's murder two years later. Incest, rape and murder—these are the fruits of love gone wrong.

We must refuse to accept the idolatry of romantic love. When radio love songs proclaim "You're all I need," we must rebuke that statement as misleading and untrue. We are multifaceted, complex beings, and no one person can ever meet all our psychological, emotional, intellectual and social expectations or needs. It is simply impossible.

Jack Balswick, a sociologist specializing in marriage and family development, writes, "One of the most unrealistic and unnecessary burdens we have placed upon the modern marriage relationship is the expectation that our spouse will fulfill all our needs. Too often we expect our husband or wife to be all things to us. The result is that the spouse feels inadequate when he or she can't meet all of our needs. A further result is jealousy when someone else is better able to fulfill just one dimension of our spouse's needs."[9]

But the solution is neither polygamy nor promiscuity. Instead, in the Christian community, our primary identity is that of members of the body of Christ. We are defined first and foremost by our relationship to Christ and his people, not by our relationship to spouse or family. It is unhealthy to expect that a romantic love will provide all our fundamental needs. Only in the area of sexuality are we to restrict ourselves to one relationship. If marriage partners did not demand that the other partner meet all of their social and relational needs, but relied upon mutually supportive relationships with other Christians, a lot of pressure would be off the marriage—and perhaps divorce and adultery would be less likely.

Re-envisioning Romance

When Martin Luther and Catherine von Bora wed, they did not do so out of romantic love. In fact, Luther wanted to marry a different woman; he did not like Catherine because he thought her too haughty.[10] However, Luther and Catherine wed as a theological statement against those who claimed celibacy to be a higher spiritual position. They contended instead that marriage was natural and not to be prohibited. But what started out as almost a marriage of convenience gradually developed into a story of realistic and authentic love.

> Both of them regarded marriage as a profession and divine vocation without the romantic expectations of love that were later to increase so enormously the number of disappointments and marital breakups. It is true that the two had not been passionately in love when they started out, but what began as fondness and gratitude for a new form of companionship developed into a firm bond of love.[11]

Perhaps we can learn from the Luthers' example. Perhaps we need to recover the sense of romantic love as secondary to obedience to God. It sounds strange to our ears to think of marrying somebody as an expression of Christian discipleship. But Martin and Catherine Luther entered into marriage not because of love for each other but because of love for God. Their common goal was to demonstrate that it was possible to serve God through the institution of marriage. This attitude enabled them to build a good marriage, and their relationship gradually developed into a genuine love for each other.

Distorted views of romantic love can be corrected by seeing God's ideal for love. According to the New Testament, the highest love is not the love between sexual partners but the love between friends. Jesus said, "No one has greater love than this, to lay down one's life for one's friends" (Jn 15:13 NRSV). Friendship is the highest virtue, not romance. Christians often reinterpret this verse with romantic love in mind, saying, "Oh, I love you so much, I would die for you." But this is not the primary meaning of the text. While romantic love may include friendship love, Jesus' point is that the greatest love is the sacrificial love of friends.

In this sense, all of us—single or married—can participate in the highest calling of sacrificial love, in loving God and loving our neighbors. Neither singles nor marrieds should be limited to expressing love only toward a romantic partner. In God's view of love, "happily ever after" is not limited to those who marry.

People who are considering marriage should see marriage not as a Western phenomenon but as a global one. For centuries, millions around the globe married not for love but by family arrangement. Most Westerners view this as an unacceptable infringement upon their freedom of choice. Yet statistics show that divorce is virtually unheard of in non-Western countries that practice arranged marriage, while in the United States more than a million marriages end in divorce every year. And a lot of arranged marriages turn out to be happy ones. As many have observed from my Asian culture, "In the West, marriage is like a boiling teakettle that is taken off the stove. It starts off hot but soon turns cold. In the East, marriage is like a dish that is placed on a hotplate. It begins cold but gradually warms up."

The vast majority of marriages in the Bible were arranged. Abraham sent a servant to find a wife for his son, Isaac. Rebekah was brought back for Isaac, and Genesis 24:67 says that Isaac married Rebekah: "So she became his wife, and he loved her." Notice the order. It does not say that Isaac fell in love with Rebekah, courted her, proposed marriage and then wed her. Rather, he married her *first* and came to love her *afterward.*

One could even say that the very first couple was an arranged marriage. After all, Eve was the only woman God created for Adam—what other options did he have? Notice that Scripture never mentions that Adam "fell in love" with Eve. He simply acknowledged her to be bone of his bone and flesh of his flesh, and he married her.[12]

Robert Fulghum, author of *All I Really Need to Know I Learned in Kindergarten,* relates this modern-day illustration from the island of Crete on the virtues of arranged marriage:

> The Cretans think romance is nice enough when it happens, but it is not a particularly good basis for marriage. . . . For Cretans, "making love" is a serious notion summarizing the process of marriage and family. When two families agree that a son and a daughter would suit one another, it is expected that over time the man and woman will work at becoming compatible partners in the same spirit one might work at achieving competence in a life's vocation. This is making love.
>
> Time and experience—mistakes and difficulties—all are part of the equation whose sum is a lasting relationship. Love is not something you fall into. Love and marriage are "made."
>
> Thus, in Cretan terms, when a married couple have been overheard arguing or fighting, the Cretans smile knowingly and say, "Ah, they are making love."[13]

John Stott observes, "The only betrothal and marriage which are described in detail in Scripture were those of Isaac and Rebekah, and this was carefully arranged (Gen 24). The western notion that 'falling in love' is the only necessary basis for marriage is quite foreign to the Bible. Most marriages in Africa and Asia today are still arranged, though usually the couple are given a veto! But parents, who have known their growing young people since birth, are likely to be the best and wisest people to choose their life partner."[14]

I am not advocating a return to family-arranged marriages, which would be highly impractical in our free, democratic society. However, instead of viewing romance as the isolated decision of the couple and no one else, perhaps we should recover the concept of couples covenanting together in the context of Christian community for the purpose of Christian service and ministry. The first family of the church could encourage couples whom they see as potentially good partners in ministry. Such relationships would not be love for the sake of the myth of romantic love, but love as a reflection of God's love for humanity.

If extreme forms of Western romantic love are love without commitment, and Eastern forms of arranged marriage are commitment without love, then perhaps a truly Christian approach would be an integration of both love and commitment. For the single, this would be expressed in a commitment to loving one's friends, neighbors and enemies; for the married person, it would be the same commitment but including the person's spouse.

This is a higher calling than the goal of the myth of romantic love. Perhaps those looking for love in all the wrong places should not be faulted for their quest for romantic love—the problem is just that they're not dreaming far enough. Many people just want to find somebody to marry. That's not enough of a goal. The wedding day is not the ultimate destination. A far higher dream is to craft together a life of service to God and love for Christ.

If this kind of life is expressed in marriage, then mutual attraction is not enough; mutual commitment is also necessary. If this is not part of the romantic dream, then the dream falls short of a Christian ideal for marriage. Too many people marry for love and later find themselves in painful and even abusive situations. It is *far better to be single than married to somebody who is bad for you.*

"Your feelings of misery as a single are nothing compared to the misery of being in a bad marriage," pastor Bill Hybels writes.[15] "The most miserable people in the world are not single people. They are married people who realize that their marriage was a mistake."[16]

The Dark Side of Dating

"I think it's hard for Christians to date," Cheryl said, "because there's a stronger desire to get married. If you do go out with someone, for a movie or dinner, you automatically start wondering right away if you are going to marry this person, and I don't know if that's good. It's hard to date as a Christian single."

Not only must we be cautious with the concept of romantic love, we must also be careful to have a healthy view of dating. Dating, in the modern sense of the practice, is not biblical. Like romantic love, dating is a Western phenomenon. It fits our consumer mentality. We shop for food, clothing, CDs and everything else; why not shop for a partner, too?

One subtle result of dating can be that we become consumers in quest of the perfect product. We are forever upgrading to the new and improved model. We're never quite content with what we have because we see so many others out there that might be better but are just slightly out of reach or beyond our budget. Dating becomes like looking for a used car. We keep on shopping around and trading up.

With this approach, people are no longer people in their own right; they are only objects that we use for our own pleasure or benefit. Their value depends on how well they meet our needs. After all, shopping is essentially a selfish activity, is it not? I shop for things that benefit *me*. And in my quest for the perfect partner, I look for somebody who will make *me* happy, who will make *me* look good, who will bring *me* fulfillment and pleasure and take away my loneliness. "It's worth noting how well the narrative of romantic love supports the ethos of late capitalism, which demands that the ideal consumer be perpetually frustrated and never really contented."[17]

On one hand, a consumerist view of dating may make us too eager to "close the deal." We can be so excited about the new car that we don't notice the rust. A relationship may have barely begun when thoughts of marriage enter in. Not enough time is spent developing a foundational friendship before romantic attachments come into view.

On the other hand, dating may prepare us for divorce. If we float from one dating partner to another, we may learn how to initiate and break off relationships without learning the concept of long-term commitment. If the relationship develops problems, we just take the person back to the exchange counter and get one that works better.

Rodney Clapp summarizes this well:

A Christian marries and commits him- or herself exclusively to a particular mate—"till death do us part." The consumer, on the other hand, marries because marriage will serve his or her interests as he or she understands them at the moment. Commitment in the Christian way of life is an ideal and a goal; commitment in the consumer way of life is more exclusively an instrumental and typically temporary good. Marriage in the consumer ethos is too often open to reevaluation. If at any point it fails to promote the self-actualization of one or another spouse, the option of ending the partnership must be available.[18]

Healthy relationships are not developed out of a promiscuous search for love and fulfillment in a multiplicity of partners. A desperate quest of just this sort can be fueled by a mistaken concept of shopping for the ideal person, leaving behind broken relationships and shipwrecked marriages—casualties of "serial monogamy."[19]

Learning to Build Relationships

Because previous generations have believed in the myth of romantic love, it has been difficult for both men and women to make genuine opposite-sex friendships. The tendency has been to initiate opposite-sex friendships only when desiring a romantic relationship. "Men and women have been taught to see one another only in the most starkly contrasting, black-and-white terms: either as lovers or as the most casual of acquaintances. . . . When people saddled with such cramped imaginations have any feelings at all for a woman or man, they are faced with only two options: go to bed or never see each other again. This isn't freedom. This is tragedy."[20]

This pattern has been changing to some extent in recent years, especially because the current generation of young adults has grown up as the first truly unisex generation.

This generation has also grown up having much closer contact between males and females, and the result is more of a friendship relationship than a mystery relationship. They know each other very well, but more like brothers and sisters. This close rapport is almost impossible for older generations to understand.

When a high school girl calls a high school boy on the phone and they talk long and often, parents assume there is a romance in progress. They simply don't believe their children when they say, "Oh, we're just friends." It is even more unbelievable when a group of young adult men and women share the same apartment and insist that there is nothing more than a platonic relationship between them. "Date" belongs to the vocabulary of their parents and grandparents. They just "do things together," often taking turns paying the check.[21]

My parents, who were born during World War II, have difficulty understanding how I am able to have friendships with women whom I am not dating. In their culture, men and women did not interact unless they were "courting." My parents object when I maintain friendships with my opposite sex friends, especially after they become engaged or married. In their minds, the fact that they are now married makes them "off limits," because the only legitimate reason for maintaining the friendship would be to pursue future romantic involvement.

This seems to me like a deficient understanding of the interrelatedness and interdependency of men and women. My parents don't understand that I was friends with these women on a purely platonic level before they got married and so we can still be friends after marriage. Certainly the interpersonal dynamic has changed, and we must be mindful of appropriate boundaries. The new spouse certainly becomes part of our friendship. But marriage should not become a barrier between friends.

This openness notwithstanding, it is still difficult to forge authentic friendships between men and women, because, as Harry says in *When Harry Met Sally,* "Men and women can't be friends because the sex part always gets in the way." Sexual tension and romantic interest from one side or the other often sabotage genuine opposite-sex friendships, especially when one person would like to pursue something beyond friendship and the other person doesn't reciprocate. Is it possible to get past the games we play with one another in our opposite-gender relationships?

The Christian gospel introduces the possibility of friendships between men and women that need not be either seductive nor manipulative. Christian men and women are first and foremost brothers and sisters in Christ. Our primary perception of each other should not be as potential husband or wife, but as brother or sister. Even if marriage someday does develop, the primary relationship between the two is still as fellow Christians.

Such a view may help demystify opposite-gender relationships. Instead of asking, "How do I understand these frustrating men," a Christian woman can ask, "How do I get along with my brother?" This in itself can eliminate a lot of the game-playing. Instead of tortuous games of playing hard-to-get, flirting, advancing and withdrawing, we can instead apply basic Christian principles of honesty, decency, openness and civility. Instead of treating someone differently because he or she is a prospective dating partner, we can treat everybody with the kind of Christian conduct we are expected to have in all situations. We can do unto others as we would have done to us.

Because we live in a fallen, imperfect world, our opposite-sex friendships and relationships will probably never be completely free of ulterior motives. Our problem in developing lasting relationships is that we try to move directly from loneliness to relationship. The usual romantic story runs like this: A young single person is lonely and dreams of sharing his or her life with someone. So he or she goes on a quest to find that person, and once that person is found, marriage takes place.

I would suggest that for a happier ending, several intermediate steps need to take place. If a young single person is lonely, then the first step is to address the loneliness and find identity and solitude in relationship with God. The next step is to meet the need for companionship not in an individual Prince Charming or Miss Right but in Christian community and fellowship. One makes friends with many people of both sexes in the context of that community. And out of those friendships, if a particular person seems to be a potential dating partner, then and only then should a dating relationship be pursued.

Too often an overambitious suitor pursues the beloved quarry at such high velocity and with such intensity that the object of affection feels smothered. When such an obvious effort is made to win someone's heart, the response is often an equal and opposite reaction. Such an approach to dating bypasses establishing a good friendship first—and sows the seeds of distrust. The subconscious question is, "Does this person really want to be my friend, or is this person just looking for somebody to date?"

A healthier approach is to develop good relational skills and focus on building good friendships. Many of today's young single adults lacked good role models for relationships due to brokenness and dysfunction in our families of origin. Therefore, it can be helpful for churches to encourage their singles to learn healthy relationship skills through classes on Christian dating and relationships. Some churches have instituted "dating counseling" as a form of pre-premarital counseling. Tim Celek and Dieter Zander write, "Busters are eager to learn how to relate to each other, because that's a life skill they frequently had little contact with as they grew up. They want to avoid the pitfalls they saw their parents blunder into. People who've had little or no exposure to Christianity say dating counseling had a great effect on them. Usually a boyfriend or girlfriend brings them."[22]

We can take other steps to learn how to build healthy friendships. A few years ago I picked up M. Blaine Smith's book *Should I Get Married?* I wasn't thinking of getting married anytime soon; I wasn't even dating anyone at the time. I just had a vague idea that I really didn't know very much about relationships. I wanted to know what constitutes a good relationship—one that could someday lead to marriage. So I started reading.

Something I soon realized was how little most people prepare for relationships. Think of how much time, education, energy and training goes into a college degree or preparation for a career. But how many people automatically know how to build good, lasting friendships, especially with those of the opposite sex? While it may seem to come naturally for some, most of us tend to have difficulty building real friendships. We have insecurities; we have trouble being vulnerable; we are shy; we lack good role models of healthy relationships. So relationships do not come naturally. Far from it. Relational skills, like everything else in life, require training. As Walter Trobisch titled his book, love is a feeling to be *learned.*

Anybody who is interested in dating should first read some good books about friendships and relationships. Alice and Bob Fryling wrote *A Handbook for Engaged Couples*[23] because they were amazed at the numbers of engaged and married couples who had never learned basic communication skills. (A good understanding of these kinds of interpersonal skills will improve all of our interactions with people, not just our dating relationships.)

Keith Anderson, campus pastor of Bethel College in Minnesota, always recommends that engaged couples get books and videos about marriage. Many times someone will say, "I can't afford to buy a book about marriage right now." Anderson responds, "Then get the book from the library, or don't get married!"[24] He points out that many young couples are willing to spend thousands of dollars on the engagement ring, wedding and honeymoon—

but unwilling to spend ten dollars on a book that may have more lasting value and benefit for their marriage than any wedding paraphernalia.

Many books (perhaps too many) have been written about building friendships and dating relationships. I encourage you to sift through the fluff and seek out quality titles.[25]

Temptations of Many Kinds

After we develop a healthy network of friendships in the context of Christian community, it's possible some of these friendships will develop into romantic relationships. If friendship leads to a dating relationship, dating may give way to opportunities for sexual temptation.

As already noted, being single does not automatically provide a supernatural gift that controls sexual drives or protects one from temptation. Singleness is *not* in itself a statement of self-control. Simply because a person is single and does not engage in sexual activity, that does not mean that he or she is a more self-controlled person. Given the chance, many otherwise seemingly self-controlled singles may discover a disturbingly low level of resolve.

Jesus and Paul did not embrace singleness for the sake of demonstrating self-control in the face of sexual temptation. "They were not celibate to prove their own mastery. They were celibate because their singleness enabled them to serve God in a way that would otherwise have been impossible."[26]

In fact, to partake in sexual activity forfeits the advantages of singleness. The single who does not practice abstinence will have a less effective life as a single. "Although he remains legally unmarried, the presence of a sexual partner in his life reintroduces the element of concern for the interests of another that Paul found among married persons. In fact, the concerns triggered by the presence of a sexual partner in the life of a single person can actually surpass what is present in marriage."[27]

Nevertheless, sexual temptation is a particularly difficult issue for the single adult. Here are some common pitfalls.

Lust. At the most basic level, sexual sin begins with lust. First John 2:16 mentions both the "lust of the flesh" and the "lust of the eyes." Though these can be manifested many different ways, emotional lust for a romantic relationship can be just as destructive as physical lust for sex. We must guard against any such unhealthy desires.

Masturbation. While Scripture makes no explicit references to masturbation, Tom Eisenman argues convincingly that Jesus himself may make a subtle allusion to it. In Matthew 5:27-29, Jesus teaches about adultery, saying that "anyone who looks at a woman lustfully has already committed adultery with her in his heart." The next two verses describe gouging out the right eye if it causes you to sin. Then the very next verse reads, "And if *your right hand* causes you to sin, cut it off and throw it away. It is better for you to lose one part of your body than for your whole body to go into hell" (Mt 5:30).

Eisenman astutely observes, "Imagine yourself sitting in that crowd. You are listening to Jesus preach. You hear him say that if you look with lust on another woman you have committed adultery in your heart. He tells you that your eye has led you into sin. He tells you that your right hand leads you into sin. If masturbation is an obsession with you, you will certainly hear a condemnation from the Lord."[28]

Pornography. Pornography takes many forms today. The sex industry has diversified far beyond *Playboy* and *Penthouse*. Besides books and magazines, there are cybersex Web pages on the Internet, CD-ROMs, pay-per-view movies and 1-976 phone sex lines. These and other kinds of pornography debase people, making them into objects to be used. And they desensitize people, destroying a healthy view of sexuality.

While pornography may tend to be a typically male temptation, a female equivalent could be called "emotional pornography." What visual pictures of scantily-clad women do for men, romance novels and soap operas can do for women. Both can be just as unhealthy. "The romantic image of the damsel swept off her feet by the white knight is no more realistic than the pornographic image of the inexperienced prude turned sex-crazed woman by a macho man."[29] An addiction to romance novels can be just as destructive as addiction to visual forms of pornography.

Prior to becoming a Christian, romance novelist Francine Rivers authored thirteen mass-market romance novels, selling about three million copies. She found herself addicted to reading and writing romance novels. According to Rivers, "Many romance readers are romance addicts. I've met people who will buy two hundred books a month, reading one after another. Many of them lack a real love relationship in their life, or are hiding from emotional pain."[30]

Other temptations. A friend went to New York City for management training. While he was walking around the city streets, he was propositioned by six or seven different prostitutes. "I could tell Satan was trying to tempt me," he said. "Think about it. A twenty-six-year-old guy, a thousand miles from home—I kept hearing a voice in my mind saying, 'No one will ever know.'"

Such lies entice us many ways. Channel surf to an erotic movie—no one will ever know. Browse through an explicit magazine—no one will ever know. Or so we deceive ourselves. When faced with so many formidable temptations, how does a single adult refrain from giving in? One single confided, "I struggle daily with issues of sexual temptation. How did Paul handle it? I would really like to know."

Toward Sexual Purity

A theology of singleness includes a healthy theology of sex. The first step to a healthy approach toward sexuality is to recognize that sexual expression is not essential for life. Robert DeMoss, a thirty-seven-year-old virgin, wrote in his book *Sex and the Single Person*, "Sex is a *drive*—not a *need*. We *need* air, food, sleep and water to exist. The sexual expression is *optional*."[31]

We must counter the societal lie that sexual expression is necessary for fulfillment in life. Our primary response, as John Stott articulates, is that

> Jesus our Lord . . . never married or experienced sexual intercourse. Yet he was and is the perfect model of humanness. His example teaches us that it is perfectly possible to be single, celibate and human at the same time![32]

Jesus himself is our example for living the single life without sexual activity. "To believe that he was unmarried is not to deny his humanity, but to affirm that the sexual congress of husband and wife is not an essential part of our humanity."[33] Rodney Clapp similarly writes:

> To live without genital expression is not to be less than a whole person. Our popular and commercial media relentlessly insist that sex will make our lives complete. Early Christians were seen to be atheists because they rejected the proposition that Caesar saves. Late-twentieth-century Christians would be little less revolutionary in their "atheism" if they now rejected the proposition that sex saves. And what bolder way to reject that proposition than to live a full and vigorous life without sex?[34]

While we acknowledge that sex is a good gift designed by God, we must also affirm that it is intended for only appropriate circumstances. Richard

Foster writes, "Sex is like a river—it is a good and wonderful blessing when kept within its proper channel."[35] According to Scripture, that proper channel is within the marriage relationship.

Believing this, single Christians may fall to yet another temptation: the temptation to believe that marriage will solve the issue of sexual temptation and sexual sin. This is simply not true. In confessing his continuing struggle with pornography, an anonymous pastor wrote, "Even marriage, Christian marriage, does not remedy lust. If anything, it complicates the problem by introducing a new set of difficulties. Lust continues to seek the attraction of unknown creatures and the taste for adventure and chance meetings."[36]

Simply put, if you are lustful as a single, you will be lustful in your marriage. Marriage does not remove impure sexual thoughts or behavior. Such things are an internal condition not dependent on whether or not you have a spouse to have sex with.

I remember an article about "emotional adultery." A single man was struggling with sexual desires and told a married man that he envied his marriage, since he could have sex anytime. The married man responded that it didn't get any easier in marriage, reflecting that though he had been physically faithful to his wife, many times he had had lustful, adulterous thoughts of other women. Marriage is no sure-fire cure for sexual sin. The Christian is to deal with sexual sin whether or not he or she ever experiences marital sex.

Our problem is not that we don't know this. Our problem is knowing how this translates into specifics. Scripture doesn't give detailed answers to questions like "how far is too far" in dating.

"I feel frustrated because I know I should be more pure in so many ways, but Bible studies are always so vague on plans of action for purity," one single said. "A lot of my problem is that a part of me really enjoys some impure things and I don't want to give them up. *How do you run from something you enjoy?*"

How can single Christians escape the bondage of sexual sin? Many books have been written on the topic, some with all sorts of specific techniques for avoiding temptation. While well-intentioned, such advice is often unhelpful. We may try with all our energy to adhere to wise, common-sense guidelines, but more often than not, we find ourselves slipping back into sin. Richard Foster describes this scenario well:

Our ordinary method of dealing with ingrained sin is to launch a frontal attack. We rely on our willpower and determination. Whatever may be the issue for us—anger, fear, bitterness, gluttony, pride, lust, substance abuse—we determine never to do it again; we pray against it, fight against it, set our will against it. But the struggle is all in vain, and we find ourselves once again morally bankrupt or, worse yet, so proud of our external righteousness that "whitened sepulchers" is a mild description of our condition.[37]

Foster then directs our attention to Paul's counsel in Colossians 2:20-23, which carries new meaning when read in light of our futile attempts to control our sexual urges:

Since you died with Christ to the basic principles of this world, why, as though you still belonged to it, do you submit to its rules: "Do not handle! Do not taste! Do not touch!"? These are all destined to perish with use, because they are based on human commands and teachings. Such regulations indeed have an appearance of wisdom, with their self-imposed worship, their false humility and their harsh treatment of the body, but they lack any value in restraining sensual indulgence.

These words resonate with our experience. Our self-imposed rules sound much like the Colossians' "Do not touch." We say instead, "Do not go farther than kissing. Do not spend too much time alone. Do not go parking. Do not lie down on a bed together. Do not undress each other." And such regulations do indeed have an appearance of wisdom. After all, we would hardly counsel teenagers to do the opposite! But the sad truth of the matter is that these regulations "lack any value in restraining sensual indulgence." Why? Because the issue is internal, not external. External stimuli may provide opportunity, but the ultimate problem is that our inner selves want to follow the lust of the flesh.

If setting forth rules doesn't help, what will? Paul does not provide a detailed list of situational dos and don'ts. Rather, he exhorts us to set our hearts and minds on things above, put to death everything that is of the earthly nature and clothe ourselves in virtue (3:1-17). We may ask him, "How do we do this?" Paul has no slick solution. Apparently he leaves it up to the Colossians to decide for themselves what to do. What is more important to Paul is that the end goal be clearly in view—ridding our lives of anger, rage, lying and the like and taking on compassion, humility, patience and so on. Perhaps Paul is a pragmatist; it may not matter as much to him what specific steps we actually take to pursue holiness and purity, as long as we choose to do so and find an approach that works for us.

The Virtue of Celibacy

Perhaps it is time to suggest a positive view of sexuality for Christian singles. Negative prohibitions can only go so far. Better to have a positive, proactive understanding and approach to sexual purity in singleness.

In the area of sexuality, Christian singles have much to learn from those who have made lifelong commitments to singleness. Vocational singles like Catholic priests, nuns and monks often have a greater depth of understanding of sexuality and celibacy than do evangelical Protestants. In *The Cloister Walk*, poet Kathleen Norris writes of her experiences living at a Benedictine monastery. During her residency, she gained an unusual appreciation of the practice of celibacy.

Celibacy is not as foreign a concept as we might think. Norris, who is married, notes that "celibacy, like monogamy, is not a matter of the will disdaining and conquering the desires of the flesh but a discipline."[38] It is no higher calling for singles to be celibate than for married couples to be monogamous. Just as married couples vow to be monogamous, these singles vow to be celibate.

Indeed, celibates may be more aware of their vows than marrieds. Churches "do not adequately convey to married people the sacredness of a lifelong commitment to another person, whereas for sisters the religious nature of their vows is an everyday reality."[39]

In this sense, celibacy can be excellent preparation for marriage. A single who is committed to celibacy will develop the discipline needed to practice fidelity in marriage. Christian singles should not feel as if celibate sexual purity is impossible to attain. If one cannot be celibate as a single, how does one expect to be faithful as a spouse?

Furthermore, a commitment to celibacy can help us develop the genuine opposite-sex friendships we yearn for. Norris notes that celibates tend to value friendships highly. Her friendships with celibate men "give me some hope that men and women don't live in alternate universes." She describes male celibacy in particular as "radically countercultural," in that it rejects societal consumerist models of sexuality:

I have never had a monk friend make an insinuating remark along the lines of, "You have beautiful eyes" (or legs, breasts, knees, elbows, nostrils), the usual catalogue of remarks that women grow accustomed to deflecting. . . . in giving up the sexual pursuit of women (whether as demons or as idealized vessels of purity), the male celibate learns to relate to them as human beings.[40]

Learning to develop celibate friendships is advantageous for singles who eventually do marry. After all, married couples must learn to relate as friends, not only as sexual partners. "It is precisely the skills of celibate friendship—fostering intimacy through letters, conversation, performing mundane tasks together (thus rendering them pleasurable), savoring the holy simplicity of a shared meal, or a walk together at dusk—that can help a marriage survive the rough spots. When you can't make love physically, you figure out other ways to do it."[41]

Committed celibates are no less human or sexual because of their vows; indeed, they are people who are "fully aware of themselves as sexual beings but who express their sexuality in a celibate way. That is, they manage to sublimate their sexual energies toward another purpose other than sexual intercourse and procreation."[42]

How do we express our sexuality in a celibate way? A commitment to celibacy challenges us to channel our sexual energies elsewhere. This is not merely exercising or jogging to work off sexual frustration. It is not accomplished by distracting ourselves with work, food, sports or television. Nor is it a denial of our sexual desires or repression of feelings. "Celibacy is not a vow to repress our feelings," a sister said. "It is a vow to put all our feelings, acceptable or not, close to our hearts and bring them into consciousness through prayer."[43]

Norris cites a prioress who spoke of "sins against celibacy" as not primarily sexual acts but emotions: "Celibacy is not an excuse for being unhappy or uncharitable, to stuff feelings down, to become angry, or an iceberg. The worst sin against celibacy is to pretend not to have any affections at all."[44]

Celibacy can be seen as a spiritual discipline that results in a more thoroughly Christian life. One nun said, "For me, the discipline of celibacy means a commitment to grow, intellectually and in my prayer life, to engage in regular prayer, both privately and with my community, to engage in some form of meaningful ministry, to take care of my body, to seek out solitude at regular intervals, and to take pleasure in beauty."[45]

A commitment to celibacy challenges us to examine ourselves deeply when we struggle with sexual temptation. For example, one nun said, "If a young sister comes to me and says that she's been masturbating, the question I want her to address is: Why? Why now? Is she lonely? . . . Is she infatuated with someone, and using this as a way to find sexual release?" If so, "the questions she'll need to ask herself, if she wants to remain a nun, are: How does Christ's love show through this person she loves? How can she best show her love in return—for the person, for the community, for Christ? Chances are it's not by masturbating."[46]

Another nun said, "The object of celibacy is consciousness, taking our unconscious feelings and sexual urges and placing them where we think God wants them."[47]

Instead of fighting an endless and losing battle against sexual temptations, a more constructive approach for Christian singles is to come to view sexual temptations as an affirmation of our identity as sexual beings—and also as a reminder of our dependence on God. Instead of a source of perpetual frustration and failure, sexual temptation can be an opportunity for prayer and spiritual growth. "Celibacy," as one sister said, "has given me a good way to integrate my sexuality with my spirituality; I've come to realize that the goal of both is union with God and with others."[48]

It is not too bizarre for Protestant single Christians to take a vow of celibacy. Perhaps our problem with sexual temptations is that we have merely assumed that we will be sexually pure without explicitly and publicly saying so. There is great merit to an intentional act, perhaps in the context of an accountability group, to which we can look back as a marker, where we say, "Here I stand; I vow to be a sexually pure single Christian." Christian teenagers by the thousands have been doing precisely this in the recent True Love Waits campaign, where they sign cards pledging to save sex for marriage. Some wear rings symbolizing their commitment to virginity and chastity.

In this way, Christian singles can stand against the tide and make a powerful statement that we will not live by cultural standards of sexuality. Instead, we will dedicate our sexuality—our bodies, minds and emotions—to God and no other.

A Community of Hope

Though sexual temptation is a personal issue, the way out from sexual temptation is not an individualistic one. Few of us have the strength to withstand temptations on our own. But if we find accountability and encouragement in the Christian community, in trusted friends to whom we can open up, we discover that we are not alone in our struggles. The body of Christ can help keep us in check when we are weak.

In the spring of 1995, God moved in a visible way at many college campuses across the U.S. Spontaneous student meetings were marked with conviction of sin and public repentance and confession. At Wheaton College, students lined up at microphones and admitted their wrongdoings from 9 p.m. until 6 a.m. They confessed their struggles with sexual activity and substance abuse as well as pride and cynicism. Students brought forward stumbling blocks in their lives: alcohol, drugs, pornography, and other items which had become idols in their lives, such as name-brand clothing. Some students cut up their credit cards; others shattered their CDs. The fruit of the confession was seen in acts of restitution. Students reimbursed the bookstore for items they had stolen and admitted to their professors that they had cheated on tests.

Several themes recurred in students' testimonies. First, they felt the need to publicly confess, to say out loud that they had wronged God and the community. Second, they asked for prayer for their struggles. Third, they asked for accountability, through close friendships, small groups or other forms of discipleship.

These three elements—confession, prayer and accountability—will help us in our struggles against sexual temptation. Ultimately, we must choose to *act* our way out of sexual temptation and immoral activity. "People do not merely talk themselves into sin; they *act*. And by the same token, I do not believe anyone ever talks himself *out* of sin. Again there must be action, and this action must involve not only confession, of an ultimately open type, but also atonement."[49]

When we break the silence and admit the dark areas we try to cover up the most, other Christians can keep us in check, pray for us, hold us accountable, encourage us and help us. We can't do it on our own. But if we are real with one another and depend on the body of Christ, we need not struggle alone.

Discussion Questions

1. What are some examples of how romantic love can be destructive? What difficulties have you encountered in dating? What steps can you

take to learn how to build healthy relationships?

2. "Far better to be single than married to somebody who is bad for you." Do you believe this?

3. Have you ever made an intentional commitment to celibacy or sexual purity? Why or why not?

4. Do you have accountability relationships to help you in your struggles? If so, how have such relationships been helpful? If not, whom might you approach to begin such a relationship?

9

TEMPTATIONS
SINGLES FACE

I can resist everything except temptation.
OSCAR WILDE

In Anne Tyler's novel *The Accidental Tourist,* single adult Julian laments living in an apartment building inhabited exclusively by singles. He says, "All the people in my apartment building eat out, and there's nothing in any of the kitchens but a couple cans of peanuts and some diet soda."[1]

Singles with underdeveloped culinary skills often fall into the habit of making do with junk-food meals. Though junk food is not exclusive to singles, many of us identify with the temptation to be undisciplined in the areas of nutrition, exercise and time management.

While the single life is not inherently more difficult than the married life, each has its own particular set of challenges. Married people have married problems: relationship maintenance, conflict resolution, financial priorities, parenting issues. Singles have singleness problems. Some of those are genuine temptations.

When dealing with temptation of any kind, our natural inclination is not to resist it. Left to our own devices, more often than not, we will make wrong choices, because we follow what we feel is the natural thing to do.

This is why many singles fall into sexual sin. They say to themselves, "But it seems so natural to just do it! It's unnatural to abstain from sex, to deny those desires and feelings!"

The answer to this point of view is to recognize that the Christian life is rarely "natural." Far from it. It is not natural to love your neighbor, or to turn the other cheek, or to forgive someone who has wronged you. In the same way, resisting sexual temptation—or any kind of temptation—is not the "natural" thing to do. Christianity runs counter to humanity's baser natural intentions. By God's grace, and with the help of the Holy Spirit and the body of Christ, Christians are called to resist what is wrong and do what is right, regardless of how "unnatural" it may seem by societal standards.

This being said, we can examine specific temptations of the single life. Some issues have already been addressed in some way or another throughout this book; for example, the temptation to think we are incomplete without a spouse can be corrected with a more biblical understanding of our identity as whole persons. The temptation to wallow in loneliness and self-pity can be resolved with the disciplines of solitude and community. Whatever our struggles may be, we can be confident that God can help us face them.

Tempted to Put Life on Hold

Many singles have the vague sense that singleness is a temporary phase, that "real life" begins at marriage. For this reason, they put life on hold, waiting until a mate comes along before really living life. Singles with this philosophy may have apartments that resemble college dorm rooms, furnished with crates and second-hand furniture. Bachelor pads are notorious for shabby decor and minimal upkeep.

But it is not true that the quality of life of those who are married is automatically better than those who are single. Marriage is not the starting point for "real life." Salvation in Christ is. And all who have come to Christ have already begun to participate in the abundant life Jesus came to bring us.

God calls us to live a productive single life, not just wait for a marriage. While it is not wrong to wait on the Lord, "waiting does not imply that we sit and do nothing. We act carefully and in accordance with God's will so far as this can be determined. Then we trust that God's plans for us will become apparent, in his timing."[2]

Taking life off hold means that we live life to the full, whether or not we have a mate. Want to see a new movie, but don't have a date? Nothing is keeping you from seeing it by yourself. We must not believe the lie that only social failures go to movies alone. No, people who refuse to put their lives on hold choose to live life in the present, making the most of every opportunity.

We can participate in ministries, go back to school, learn a new language, find a new hobby, see a new play, or pursue whatever interests our hearts may desire. We need not "save up" our vital life experiences for a future marriage. One author writes, "Take your life off hold! Open up that hope chest. Pull out the dishes, the silver pitcher and the tea set and put them to good use with some old-fashioned hospitality. Dig your life out of the hopes for tomorrow and invest it in the realities of today. Stop waiting and start living!"[3]

A turning point in Linda's life came when she decided to purchase a sofa for the living room of her apartment. She had previously thought, "I can't get a sofa. That's what married people do. I'm not married; I can't get one yet." But then she realized that if she got married, she could bring the sofa to the marriage, or she could sell it. Buying the sofa became a way for Linda to stop putting her life on hold.

The same principle applies to purchasing a house. In the U.S. at present, owning a home and accumulating equity usually makes more sense than paying rent year after year. If finances permit, there is no reason for you to live in an apartment forever. It's not true that only married people buy homes and single folks should not.

Taking life off hold applies not only to material or financial investments but to social and emotional ones as well. Many singles hesitate to invest emotional energy in personal relationships, church or community because they want to "save" themselves for a future spouse. This temptation to avoid permanence only prevents us from having an abundant and fruitful life in the present.

"My first love is God," Kelly said, "and if he chooses to bring someone into my life, then he does so, but I'm not waiting around until he does. It's not like I'll get value or importance as soon a man enters my life. I'm comfortable with where I am and what God's doing in my life."

Tempted to Be Overcommitted

One myth of singleness is that singles have huge amounts of free time. We hear things like, "Well, you don't have a spouse and children to take care of, so you have time to direct the children's Christmas musical, right?"

On the contrary, singles tend to be just as busy as married people, if not more so. It's simply a reality of modern life that everybody, whether married or single, is easily consumed by too many things to do—work, meetings, community events, errands, committees or church activities. The single person's schedule can be just as filled, even if the daily planner doesn't include picking up kids from day care or after-school extracurriculars.

Part of our busyness is that so much of our time is invested in building friendships. Because our primary relationships and parafamily often come from friends who usually don't live under the same roof, it takes more time and effort to maintain them.

Often singles feel that others monopolize their time. "I might have more time to myself, but it gets filled up by people who *think* I have more time," said Amy.

In fact, singles may juggle too many responsibilities precisely because they don't have a spouse and family. Singles don't have a spouse to help handle the little details of daily life. You can't ask someone else to do the laundry or take out the garbage or pay the bills or file the taxes. If the car breaks down, you don't have a spouse with another car to cover for you.

Married people have an automatic escape valve if they have too many demands; they can turn down requests because "I need to spend more time with my family. I shouldn't volunteer for this because I need to go to my son's band concert and take my daughter to volleyball practice . . ."

Singles have no such escape valve. Because we don't have family to go home to, we tend to say yes to anything that we are asked to do or participate in. The very freedoms we have to travel, to stay out late and so on end up being detrimental because they enable us to pack our schedules to unhealthy levels. Working twelve-hour days every week is probably not healthy for anyone, regardless of marital status. But nobody asks the single person, "Honey, could you spend more time at home with us?" So singles fall into traps of workaholism, stress and burnout. While married people who are overcommitted hurt their families, singles who are overcommitted only hurt themselves.

To counteract being overly busy, we must intentionally build margin into our schedules much as married people make time for their families. Pretend you have a spouse you haven't seen all day whom you need to go home and spend time with. Don't schedule the extra appointment when your days are already too long. It's okay to say no to things. Create personal time for yourself to cultivate solitude.

A principle I have found helpful is to do things not because we are driven, but because we are called. Think of the difference between a cattle driver beating and driving a herd of cows, in contrast with the image of a gentle Shepherd calling his sheep. What an encouraging metaphor—I would much rather do things knowing that Jesus is calling me to do them, not because the world is driving me.

Tragically, Christians are often just as busy and stressed-out as everybody else in our frenzied society. It seems to me that as Christians we could have a stronger witness if we weren't as frenzied in the rat race and our lives evidenced more of the peace and calm of Christ.

It is true that different personality types view these things differently; some of my friends would be in utter chaos without their daily planners. My analysis is that planners tend to contribute to workaholism, because the absence of something written in a certain time slot implies that it's free for yet another activity, when in fact it might be healthier to leave it open entirely. The knee-jerk reaction to an open planner space is that it should be filled.

A planner may not itself be the problem, but overdependence on a planner may be symptomatic of a life that needs to be reexamined. I try to keep as much in my head as possible, so I'm not crippled if I don't have my calendar with me. Henry David Thoreau said, "Simplicity, simplicity, simplicity! I say, let your affairs be as two or three, and not a hundred or a thousand; instead of a million count half a dozen, and keep your accounts on your thumb nail."[4]

In fact, some say that the goal of using an organizer is to get our lives in order to the point where we don't need the organizer. Daily planners, appointment books and other such scheduling calendars are only tools to help us. They should not run our lives or become a crutch. Think how liberating it would be to have your life so organized and in control that you didn't need to consult your Day-Timer for your every detail!

Time management is too large a topic to address here, and there are many other good resources for guidance in time management. But the goal is to avoid chronic busyness in a way that works for you. As Charles Hummel says in his classic booklet, don't let the "tyranny of the urgent" crowd out what is truly important.[5]

Tempted to Be Self-Centered

"Apart from sexual temptation," John Stott says, "the greatest danger which I think we face is self-centeredness. We may live alone, and have total freedom to plan our own schedule, with nobody else to modify it or even give us advice. If we are not careful, we may find the whole world revolving around ourselves."[6]

Because we singles often only have ourselves to think of, we tend to live fairly independent lives. We are free to settle major decisions by ourselves, without consulting a spouse or family. However, independence may turn into self-indulgence. Our schedule may be filled with items that benefit only ourselves, with little thought for others. We may be tempted to watch too much TV, spend too much money on ourselves, and forget about other people's needs.

The antidote for living in selfish ways is to become intentional about how we manage our resources, whether time, money or relationships. We must ask ourselves, "What am I doing to love my neighbor? What can I do to focus less on myself and more on others?"

Some of us may have the opposite temptation. We may focus so much on others' needs that we neglect ourselves. We must seek balance, finding healthy ways to take care of our own needs as well as looking beyond ourselves to the needs of the world around us.

A specific temptation is the temptation not to give financially. Singles who lack permanence may never get around to giving to their local church because they don't feel rooted enough to contribute. I remember worship services when not one person out of an entire row of singles put anything in the offering plate (myself included).

This may be a particularly strong temptation to singles, especially young adults who struggle to make ends meet week by week. But we should not delude ourselves into thinking that we will give more someday when we have more money and can afford it. Financial adviser Larry Burkett points out, "Most of the giving in America is not done by those with the greatest surpluses. A survey conducted for the National Family Council in 1989 showed that those with incomes above $100,000 annually gave about 2 percent of their incomes. Those with incomes between $10,000 and $50,000 gave about 5 percent."[7]

When I attended the Urbana 93 student mission convention, I was fortunate to have scholarships that covered most of my costs. This left me with extra pocket money, so I splurged at the InterVarsity Press bookstore, buying dozens of books (all on sale, of course) and a sweatshirt or two.

Then a speaker described the financial need of Christian student movements around the world. He observed that most of us delegates had spent a large amount of money on themselves that week. He challenged us to give as much to an offering for worldwide student mission as we had spent on ourselves. Yikes!

This global perspective challenged my stewardship habits. It was sobering to realize that many people in the world (if not most) do not make as much money in an entire year as I had spent on myself that week. For example, the average annual income in Mozambique is $80 US a year.[8]

On the whole we are a very wealthy people. We have been blessed with much and should be willing to give much in return, in gratitude and worship, for the purposes of ministry and meeting others' needs. If we spend more money going out to eat after church on Sunday than we are giving to meet the needs of the church and the world, something is wrong. If God blesses us with more than we need to live on, we ought to look for opportunities to give the surplus away. We can be the means by which God blesses others.

Tempted to Be Unaccountable

At a 1996 Promise Keepers rally in Minneapolis, Bruce Wilkinson of Walk Thru the Bible asked the crowd of 60,000 men, "How many of you are not in an accountability relationship with other men? Stand up, if you aren't regularly meeting with other guys who check up on you and keep you accountable." Approximately three-fourths of the men in the stadium stood.

When most people lived in small-town or rural communities, local neighborhoods were close-knit enough that everybody knew everybody else. Neighbors looked out for each other's kids. Adolescents refrained from looking at dirty magazines at the drugstore because anybody who saw them would tell their parents. Such communities kept people's moral behavior in check because of unwritten, agreed-upon standards of conduct. People in these communities held each other accountable, even though in indirect ways.

Times have changed. Suburbanization has led to a society where anonymity is the rule. Nobody frowns upon us if we rent a risqué movie or purchase contraceptives. Nobody knows us from the next person, and we are free to go about our business without any sense of shame or guilt. We live private, unaccountable lives.

But we should remember that sinful behavior will eventually come to light one way or another (Lk 12:2-3). Our hidden vices hurt ourselves and those we are close to. Furthermore, we are not meant to live isolated lives, unaccountable to anybody.

We need other Christians to help us by being our conscience for us when we ignore our own. Our temptation to do what we shouldn't can be alleviated to some extent if we know that other Christian friends are willing to ask us tough questions about how we're doing.[9] We need to have friendships with trusted confidants with whom we can share our struggles with sin and temptation.

The Promise Keepers movement rightly emphasizes this need for accountability. Promise number two of the seven promises states, "A Promise Keeper is committed to pursuing vital relationships with a few other men, understanding that he needs brothers to help him keep his promises." By making such a commitment, Promise Keepers is attempting to destroy the radical individualism that keeps men alone in their struggles. All Christians, male and female, single and married, *need* the help of other Christians to hold us accountable to the promises we make to God, ourselves and each other. We can't do it on our own.

I remember reading about a study that found that one in four youth pastors were participating in what they called "high-risk" activities, including involvement with pornography, drug or alcohol abuse or improper sexual behavior. The common denominator of these at-risk youth pastors was that none of them were accountable to anybody else for their actions. Their churches didn't have anybody checking up on them to help them with their struggles.

One-on-one mentoring relationships or a group of close friends to share with can be the best way to find accountability. Accountability has the dual purpose of keeping people from what is wrong and encouraging them to do what is right. Dan had a group of friends who would meet for the purpose of "sin maintenance," keeping each other out of sin, as well as "vision maintenance," keeping each other's visions for their lives alive. He said, "I found it absolutely invaluable to have people around me who will keep me accountable, who will chew on me and tell me, 'Dan, that is not the way to do it! Shape up!'"

Such accountability relationships require commitment, confidentiality and consistency. There must be a mutual commitment to each other's spiritual well-being. Confidentiality is essential in order to develop bonds of trust. And for an accountability relationship to be of practical good, the parties involved must meet regularly, as in a weekly Bible study or prayer-partner time. Such accountability will not only guard against various temptations and self-centeredness; it will also provide an antidote to isolation and loneliness.

Tempted to Have Lousy Holidays

Anyone who knows me will tell you that I cherish my unmarried state. I'm female, twice divorced, no kids, and no close family ties. I'm a private detective by trade. Usually I'm perfectly content to do what I do. There are times when I work long hours on a case and times when I'm on the road and times when I hole up in my tiny apartment and read books for days. When the holidays come around, however, I find that I have to exercise a certain cunning lest the absence of loved ones generate unruly depression.[10]

Singles have always faced the holidays with trepidation. It may seem like a no-win situation. If we go home to visit the folks, we face questions like, "So, are you seeing anyone?" But if we don't spend the holidays with family, we may find ourselves alone since everybody else is with their families. Enter loneliness and depression.

Sometimes it doesn't even help for families to invite singles over to share in their holiday celebrations. It may feel as if they are taking pity on poor, unfortunate orphans without a place to call home. "It's nice that people invite you to dinner, but it actually makes you feel worse," Tom said. "They're doing their family things, and you feel out of place, like you're intruding. It just reminds you that you don't have a family of your own." So while families may have good intentions, the effect may actually be to remind the single of his or her singleness even more.

In a Dear Abby column, "Single in Long Beach" had written to complain about how singles are neglected during the holidays. This prompted further letters, such as "Single in North Carolina" who spent Thanksgiving home alone watching five hours of *Gone with the Wind*. She received a phone call from another single who ate alone in a deli. A widow lamented that all her friends had abandoned her after her husband's death.

In contrast, a single wrote:

I learned long ago that no one is responsible for my loneliness but me. Why doesn't "Single" invite a friend and his family, another single, or an older couple to his home for the holidays? If he doesn't like to cook, most grocery stores and many restaurants cook turkeys with all the trimmings for carryout.

If entertaining isn't his thing, he could visit patients in nursing homes or hospitals, or lend a hand to churches and organizations that serve meals to the homeless. They appreciate all the help they can get.

Loneliness is a choice, not a necessity. Choose instead to help some of the many people who need you. *Single, but not lonely, in Alabama.*[11]

Singles in my church often get together for meals on holidays, providing fellowship for those who are without places to go. We have also spent holidays volunteering together at soup kitchens and homeless shelters.

Valentine's Day is another case. Singles don't need to be reminded that February 14 can be one of the most difficult days of the year. In fact, more suicides occur on Valentine's Day than any other day of the year except Christmas.

Few people realize that this day is named after a Christian, Valentine, who lived in Rome in the third century. Tradition has it that he was both a priest and physician who went about doing good deeds in imitation of Christ. He was arrested during a persecution of Christians, and the Roman emperor Claudius Gothicus handed him over to a magistrate. While in custody, Valentine healed the magistrate's blind, adopted daughter, and the entire family was converted to Christianity. Upon hearing this, the emperor had Valentine beheaded—on February 14. From then on Christians commemorated that day in memory of Valentine's life of selfless service and ministry.

You don't have to have a romantic partner to celebrate Valentine's Day; card stores have Valentine's Day cards for friends and family, too. Every year I buy a pack of children's valentines and give them to my friends and coworkers to let them know that I appreciate their friendship. This can be a simple way to encourage others. One year I gave a card to Liezl, a student from the Philippines, who had never celebrated a Valentine's Day before. She sent me a thank-you card in return, pleased that I had included her and helped her experience this holiday.

So commemorate this holiday by being other-centered and honoring others in the spirit of Christian love. Don't squander the day wallowing in self-pity. Don't be resentful of couples who are oblivious to anything but each other. And don't wear black all day as a protest statement. Use the day as an opportunity to write somebody you haven't heard from for a while, and let that person know you're thinking of him or her. Buy a box of chocolates and share them with friends or coworkers. Honor Christ by serving him, in the spirit of St. Valentine.

Tempted to Live a Life of Regret

We can't change the past, and we can do little to control the future, but we can choose to view the totality of our lives in a positive light. Maybe we look back and see mistakes we have made. That's okay; they're behind us now, and we can learn from them. Our mistakes are not fatal, and God is redemptive. But it's not productive to dwell on the past. You can't drive a car safely if you're eyes are glued on the rearview mirror.

Instead, we can thank God for graciously bringing us this far in our lives. We can be thankful for the experiences we've had, the friends we've made, the opportunities we've enjoyed. We can recognize that every good and perfect gift comes from God (Jas 1:17), that he is the source of all of life's blessings and our response to that should be gratitude, not bitterness or regret. If we remember that marriage is not the epitome of human experience, we need not feel that we have missed out on life.

The challenge for all of us, single or married, is to live the life we have been given, without fear or regret. Addressing singles, Tournier writes:

God loves us all . . . he wants us all to find fulfillment in our lives . . . whatever our circumstances, our frustrations, and our sufferings, he has a purpose for us, for our complete fulfillment in this life of ours, whatever it may be. To live this real life—and not dream of a different one— and to seek to live it under God is to fulfill our human destiny, a great adventure directed by God.[12]

Jesus said that those who leave behind homes and family to follow him will be honored for their sacrifice and will receive much more in the age to come (Lk 18:29-30). For today's singles, his words are a reminder that we need not live life with regret, since God will make all things new and provide us with eternal rewards far greater than the temporal experiences of having a spouse or children. Following Jesus is an adventure beyond any other, and the benefits we receive far outweigh the things we give up and the dreams we leave behind.

Discussion Questions

1. Which of the temptations mentioned do you identify with? Are there others that weren't addressed?

2. How do you manage your time and money? Are there steps you could take to get better control?

3. Do you have people who can hold you accountable and help you handle these temptations?

4. Have holidays been difficult for you? What can you do to have good holiday experiences?

5. How can you live a life without regrets?

EPILOGUE: A VISION
FOR THE FUTURE

*The man who goes alone can start today; but he who travels with
another must wait until the other is ready.*
HENRY DAVID THOREAU

At the end of a courtroom drama story, the protagonist wins the
case but loses the romance. At the end of the book he finds himself alone
on a beach, watching the sun set into the Pacific Ocean. The book concludes, "This kind of sunset demanded both a hero and a heroine, he
thought, two loving and triumphant people walking off together hand in
hand. But maybe that wasn't the only happy ending. Maybe it was just as
important to enjoy some sunsets alone . . ."[1]

At the time of Christ, the religious leaders of the day presumed that
those most acceptable to God were Jewish, male, free citizens and married.
Gentiles and Samaritans were despised, women and slaves had little value,
and single people had no place in society.

Jesus entered that culture and turned those ideas on their head. He
inaugurated a new society where one's status before God was not dependent on earthly distinctions. Jew or Greek, slave or free, male or female—
and married or single—all could now equally find their identity and fulfillment in Christ Jesus.

Our task in this book has been to explore what it means to be Christian and single, and in so doing to develop a practical theology of singleness. We have challenged traditional views that have relegated singles to a second-class status. We have seen that there is more to life than believing in the myth of romantic love, that the Western fairy tale of a married "happily ever after" is not the only paradigm for a successful life. "The faithful single . . . is a living sign that all Christians' ultimate trust and approval comes from God, not posterity."[2]

After the Urbana 96 student mission convention, some students provided feedback about what God had been doing in their lives. Several wrote that they had come to recognize that singleness could play a major role in their service to God. One said, "I learned that there are abundant blessings in my life (e.g., singleness, youth) that I have treated as downfalls, but God wants me to see and use them as gifts." Another wrote that she will go wherever God calls her to go—even if it costs her her hopes and dreams for marriage and family.

These singles had come to recognize that marriage is not the highest calling for the Christian. Indeed, singles at the crossroads can choose the way of the cross—the path of single-minded, Christian discipleship that demonstrates to the world that following Christ is the highest calling and greatest adventure for all people, single or married.

The only "special calling" Paul recognizes is the calling to be the Lord's servant. A person can answer that call in any condition—circumcised or uncircumcised, slave or free, married or single. Single people may marry if they wish—but they are equally free to stay single. The only thing that matters is living obediently before God.[3]

Dream with me of a future, of what could be—

* Singles who see their singleness as an opportunity instead of a curse, who are not halves looking for another half, but whole persons who are complete in their identity in Christ . . .

* Parents and families who celebrate the fact that their single adult children are able to serve God in ways that their married children cannot . . .

* Christian communities where singles build friendships, find support and encouragement, accountability and security . . .

* Churches that are sensitive to the needs of singles, intentional about ministering to singles, accepting and affirming singles, welcoming them as full partners in community and ministry, providing opportunities for

them to serve and use their gifts in the life of the church . . . churches where singles and married couples interact, understanding that singles and families need each other . . .

* A society where Christian singles no longer fear being alone in the world, but rather have a message of hope for the world . . .

We who are single have the opportunity and the freedom to help bring these dreams into reality. Above all else, Christian singles can demonstrate to the world that the most important thing in life is not whether or not one is married, but whether or not one knows God. "God offers His promises of joy and peace and satisfaction to anyone—married or unmarried—who has a relationship with Him."[4]

We can encourage other singles to live the dynamic lives God intends for us. In so doing, we can help the entire body of Christ become what God wants it to be. May God's kingdom come, and may his will be done on earth, as it is in heaven.

Let us put our lives on hold no longer. Let us start today.

....

APPENDIX:
JOHN STOTT ON
SINGLENESS

While conducting the research for this book, I heard that John R. W. Stott would be speaking at the InterVarsity Christian Fellowship chapter of the University of Michigan—Ann Arbor. I went there and introduced myself to Dr. Stott. I asked him if he would be willing to share his thoughts about singleness with me. Over lunch, he spoke about his views and experiences as a lifelong single. When this book was accepted for publication, my editor approached John Stott to ask permission to print the transcript as this appendix. Not only did he graciously accept, he revised and expanded his candid remarks into a more thorough treatment of the subject. The following is his material.

AH: What is your view of singleness?

JRWS: I wonder if you would allow me to postpone my answer to this question. The reason is that I think we need to discuss marriage before we discuss singleness. The refrain in Genesis 1, day by day, was "God saw that it was good." Then suddenly in Genesis 2:18 God said, "It is not good for the man to be alone." What? Something not good in God's good creation?

Yes, it is not good for human beings to be or live on their own. Calvin rightly commented that the application of this verse is wider than marriage; nevertheless, it refers primarily to marriage and so indicates that God's general will for his human creation is marriage. We single people must not resist this truth. Marriage is the norm, singleness the abnorm.

AH: What, then, is the place of singleness?

JRWS: I'm nearly ready to give you a straight answer to your question! But first I have one more point to make. This is that we must never exalt singleness (as some early church fathers did, notably Tertullian) as if it were a higher and holier vocation than marriage. We must reject the ascetic tradition which disparages sex as legalized lust, and marriage as legalized fornication. No, no. Sex is the good gift of a good Creator, and marriage is his own institution.

AH: And singleness?

JRWS: If marriage is good, singleness is also good. It's an example of the balance of Scripture that, although Genesis 2:18 indicates that it is good to marry, 1 Corinthians 7:1 (in answer to a question posed by the Corinthians) says that "it is good for a man not to marry." So both the married and the single states are "good;" neither is in itself better or worse than the other.

AH: What are the reasons for people to remain single?

JRWS: I doubt if we could find a clearer answer to this question than in the recorded teaching of Jesus himself in Matthew 19:11-12. He was talking about "eunuchs," meaning people who remain single and celibate. He listed three reasons why people do not marry.

First, for some it is "because they were born that way." This could include those with a physical defect or with a homosexual orientation. Such are congenitally unlikely to marry.

Second, there are those who "were made that way by men." This would include victims of the horrible ancient practice of forcible castration. But it would also include all those today who remain single under any compulsion or external circumstance. One thinks of a daughter who feels under obligation to forego marriage in order to care for her elderly parents.

Third, "others have renounced marriage because of the kingdom of heaven." These people, who are under no pressure from within or without, voluntarily put marriage aside, either temporarily or permanently, in order to undertake some work for the kingdom which demands single-minded devotion.

AH: Do you then regard singleness as a gift from God?

JRWS: Yes. It's noteworthy that Jesus himself, before listing those three categories of single people, said that not everybody could accept what he was about to say, "but only those to whom it has been given." If singleness is a gift, however, so is marriage. Indeed, I have myself found help in 1 Corinthians 7:7. For here the apostle writes: "each man [or woman] has his [or her] own gift from God; one has this gift, another has that." "Gift" translates *charisma*, which is a gift of God's grace (*charis*). So whether we are single or married, we need to receive our situation from God as his own special grace-gift to us.

AH: Do you mean that singleness is a gift in the sense that we are given supernatural power to cope with it?

JRWS: Not really. The gift of singleness is more a vocation than an empowerment, although to be sure God is faithful in supporting those he calls (1 Thess 5:24). Gift and calling go together. For if he calls us to singleness, the single state becomes a gift that we receive at his hand.

AH: If God calls us to singleness, does he expect us to take a vow of celibacy?

JRWS: No, I don't think so. It is true that in the Catholic tradition nuns, monks and priests take a vow of celibacy. But I question the wisdom of this. One can be celibate without taking a vow.

AH: Can you tell me about your own calling to remain single?

JRWS: Gladly. In spite of rumors to the contrary, I have never taken a solemn vow or heroic decision to remain single! On the contrary, during my twenties and thirties, like most people, I was expecting to marry one day. In fact, during this period I twice began to develop a relationship with a lady who I thought might be God's choice of life partner for me. But when the time came to make a decision, I can best explain it by saying that I lacked an assurance from God that he meant me to go forward. So I drew back. And when that had happened twice, I naturally began to believe that God meant me to remain single. I'm now seventy-six and well and truly "on the shelf"! Looking back, with the benefit of hindsight, I think I know why. I could never have traveled or written as extensively as I have done if I had had the responsibilities of a wife and family.

AH: It is widely said that without marriage sexual self-control is impossible.

JRWS: I know that this is often said. And I have to agree both that human sexual desires can be very strong, and that they are made stronger still by the pressures of the sex-obsessed culture in which we live in the West. But we Christians must insist that self-control is possible. We have to learn to control our temper, our tongue, our greed, our jealousy, our pride: why should it be thought impossible to control our libido? To say that we cannot is to deny our dignity as human beings and to descend to the level of animals, which are creatures of uncontrolled instinct.

AH: Could you give us some help in developing sexual self-control?

JRWS: It seems to me that the best advice comes from the lips of Jesus himself in the Sermon on the Mount, where he spoke of plucking out an offending eye and cutting off an offending foot. That is to say, if temptation comes through our eyes, we should not look; if through our feet (places we visit) we should not go (Mt 5:28-30). We need to be ruthless in dealing with the first approaches of sin. The New Testament calls this process "mortification." Here is the apostle Paul's most outspoken statement of it: "If you live according to the sinful nature, you will die; but if by the Spirit you put to death the misdeeds of the body, you will live" (Rom 8:13). In other words, what the world calls life (self-indulgence) is in reality death, whereas putting to death whatever is sinful within us (self-denial) is in reality life. It is what Jesus called "taking up the cross"; it has to be done *daily* (Lk 9:23).

AH: Another argument I have heard is that sexual self-control is not only impossible but actually dehumanizing, since sexual intercourse is supposedly an indispensable aspect of human experience.

JRWS: Yes, I have heard this argument too. In fact, the Corinthian false teachers seem to have used it in a letter to Paul. One of their slogans was "food for the stomach and the stomach for food" (1 Cor 6:13). They were probably saying that just as food and the stomach are meant for each other, so are the body and sex. The stomach can't survive without food; just so the body can't survive without sex. It's a specious argument, but a blatant lie, which we need to have the courage to repudiate. Jesus our Lord (in the nature of the case) never married or experienced sexual intercourse. Yet he was and is the perfect model of humanness. His example teaches us that it is perfectly possible to be single, celibate and human at the same time!

AH: Do you struggle with loneliness?

JRWS: Yes, certainly. God created us as social beings. Love is the greatest thing in the world. For God is love, and when he made us in his own image, he gave us the capacity to love and to be loved. So we need each other. Yet marriage and family are not the only antidotes to loneliness.

Let me tell you some of my own experiences in this area. To begin with, some pastors work on their own, isolated from their peers, and in consequence are lonely. But the New Testament plainly envisages that each local church will have a *plural* oversight. See, for example, Acts 14:23 and Titus 1:5. So in All Souls Church in the heart of London we have always had a team ministry, and we have found it an enormous enrichment. I have also been greatly blessed by Frances Whitehead, my faithful secretary for more than forty years, and by the "apostolic succession" of my study assistants. My current one is John Yates III from Falls Church, Virginia. We form a "happy triumvirate" and much appreciate the chance to work together and support each other.

In addition, single people are wise to develop as many friendships as possible, with people of all ages and both sexes. For example, although I have no children of my own, I have hundreds of adopted nephews and nieces all over the world, who call me "Uncle John." I cherish these affectionate relationships; they greatly lessen, even if they do not altogether deaden, occasional pangs of loneliness.

AH: What are the main dangers to which single people are exposed?

JRWS: Apart from sexual temptation, to which I have already referred, the greatest danger which I think we face is self-centeredness. We may live alone and have total freedom to plan our own schedule, with nobody else to modify it or even give us advice. If we are not careful, we may find the whole world revolving around ourselves. So I have found it helpful to have six or eight friends, who are known as "AGE" (Accountability Group of Elders), with whom I meet several times a year, and whose advice I seek about my schedule, and especially about which invitations I should accept.

AH: What then are the liberties which singleness brings?

JRWS: Paul gives a straight answer to this question. Unmarried people, he wrote, are "concerned about the Lord's affairs," how they can please him, whereas married people are "concerned about the affairs of this world," how they can please their spouse, and consequently their interests are divided (1 Cor 7:32-34). Single people experience the great joy of being able to devote themselves, with concentration and without distraction, to the work of the Lord.

AH: Would you ever advise a single person to seek an arranged marriage?

JRWS: Yes, in some circumstances I think I would. After all, the only betrothal and marriage which are described in detail in Scripture were those of Isaac and Rebekah, and this was carefully arranged (Gen 24). The Western notion that "falling in love" is the only necessary basis for marriage is quite foreign to the Bible. Most marriages in Africa and Asia today are still arranged, though usually the couple are given a veto! But parents, who have known their growing young people since birth, are likely to be the best and wisest people to choose their life partner.

AH: Do you have a final word of advice for single people?

JRWS: Yes! First, don't be in too great a hurry to get married. We human beings do not reach maturity until we are about twenty-five. To marry before this runs the risk of finding yourself at twenty-five married to somebody who was a very different person at the age of twenty. So be patient. Pray daily that God will guide you to your life partner or show you if he wants you to remain single. Second, lead a normal social life. Develop many friendships. Third, if God calls you to singleness, don't fight it. Remember the key text: "Each person has his or her own gift of God's grace" (1 Cor 7:7).

Notes

Why This Book?
[1]Gary Collins, *Christian Counseling,* rev. ed. (Waco, Tex.: Word, 1988), p. 365.

Chapter 1: Where Singles Are Today
[1]Jenell Williams, "On Soup Cans and Marilyn Monroe: Christianity, Feminism, and the Challenges of Postmodernism," *Regeneration Quarterly* 1 (Fall 1995): 18.

[2]Carolyn A. Koons and Michael J. Anthony, *Single Adult Passages* (Grand Rapids, Mich.: Baker Book House, 1991), p. 48.

[3]More precise statistics are married, spouse present, 53.4%; married, spouse absent, 3.5%; widowed, 6.6%; divorced, 8.9%; single (never married) 27.5%. From U.S. Bureau of the Census, "Current Population Survey: March 1996" (Washington: U.S. Government Printing Office, September 1996).

[4]Pamela Cytrynbaum, "Today's singles are looking for match made in cyberspace," *Chicago Tribune,* October 25, 1995, p. 15.

[5]Numbers are from U.S. Bureau of the Census, *Statistical Abstract of the United States, 1992,* cited in William Bennett, *The Index of Leading Cultural Indicators* (New York: Simon & Schuster, 1994), p. 56.

[6]Ibid.

[7]U.S. Bureau of the Census, "Current Population Survey: March 1996."

[8]U.S. Bureau of the Census, in Famighetti, *World Almanac 1996,* p. 391, and Otto Johnson, ed., *Information Please Almanac 1996* (New York: Houghton Mifflin, 1995), p. 835.

[9]Cited in *Leadership Journal,* Summer 1996, p. 69. For a similar perspective but with different numbers, see George Barna, *The Future of the American Family* (Chicago: Moody, 1993), p. 67; "The people who get divorced and who get married this year are, for the most part, different people. It is not possible to claim that half of all marriages end in divorce simply because we had two times as many people get married as got divorced. . . . About one-quarter of all adults who marry eventually become divorced."

[10]Barna, *Future of the American Family,* pp. 119-21.

[11]U.S. Bureau of the Census, "Current Population Survey: March 1996."

[12]U.S. Bureau of the Census, "Marital Status and Living Arrangements: March 1994," *Current Population Reports,* Series P20-484.

[13]Koons and Anthony, *Single Adult Passages,* p. 48.

[14]Ibid., pp. 48-50.

[15]U.S. Bureau of the Census, "Estimated Median Age at First Marriage, by Sex: 1890 to the

Present," *Current Population Reports,* Series P20-484.

[16]Ibid.

[17]"America's Best Graduate Schools," *U.S. News and World Report,* March 20, 1995, pp. 77, 96.

[18]Barna, *Future of the American Family,* p. 49.

[19]"twentysomething," *Time,* July 16, 1990, p. 57.

[20]The term "Generation X" was popularized by the title of Douglas Coupland's 1991 novel *Generation X: Tales for an Accelerated Culture* (New York: St. Martin's Press, 1991). "Baby busters" are those who follow the baby boom generation born from 1946 to 1964; busters were born from 1965 to 1985. Sociologists William Strauss and Neil Howe call this generation of young adults "thirteeners" because they are the thirteenth generation in American history. They identify thirteeners as born between 1961 and 1981. See Strauss and Howe, *Generations: The History of America's Future 1584 to 2069* (New York: William Morrow, 1991) and *13th Gen: Abort, Retry, Ignore, Fail?* (New York: Vintage, 1993).

[21]Gary Collins and Tim Clinton, *Baby Boomer Blues* (Waco, Tex.: Word, 1992), p. 96.

[22]Tom Lasswell and Marcia Lasswell, *Marriage and the Family* (Belmont, Calif.: Wadsworth Publishing, 1987), p. 167, cited in Neil Clark Warren, *Finding the Love of Your Life* (Colorado Springs, Colo.: Focus on the Family, 1992), p. 13.

[23]Koons and Anthony, *Single Adult Passages,* p. 53.

[24]M. Blaine Smith, *Should I Get Married?* (Downers Grove, Ill.: InterVarsity Press, 1990), p. 13.

[25]Coupland, *Generation X,* p. 139.

[26]Leith Anderson, *Dying for Change* (Minneapolis, Minn.: Bethany, 1991), p. 106.

[27]Barna, *Future of the American Family,* p. 137.

[28]Bill Hybels and Rob Wilkins, *Tender Love* (Chicago: Moody, 1993), p. 26.

[29]Koons and Anthony, *Single Adult Passages,* pp. 142-43.

[30]Barna, *Future of the American Family,* p. 107.

[31]Ibid., p. 135.

[32]U.S. Bureau of the Census, "Marital Status and Living Arrangements: March 1994."

[33]Barna, *Future of the American Family,* p. 131.

[34]Koons and Anthony, *Single Adult Passages,* p. 141.

[35]Barna, *Future of the American Family,* p. 51.

[36]Jon Hassler, *North of Hope* (New York: Ballantine Books, 1990), p. 7.

[37]Cathy Guisewite, *Cathy,* Universal Press Syndicate, November 26, 1995.

[38]David Johnson, "The Pain of Porneia: Singleness and Sexuality, part 1," sermon at Church of the Open Door, Minneapolis, Minn., February 21, 1993.

[39]James Breckenridge and Lillian Breckenridge, *What Color Is Your God? Multicultural Education in the Church* (Wheaton, Ill.: Victor, 1995), p. 172.

[40]Deborah Tannen, *You Just Don't Understand* (New York: Ballantine, 1990), p. 26.

[41]Richard North Patterson, *The Final Judgment* (New York: Knopf, 1995), p. 92.

[42]Barbara Holland, *One's Company: Reflections on Living Alone* (New York: Ballantine, 1992), pp. 11-12.

[43]Koons and Anthony, *Single Adult Passages,* p. 92.

[44]Cited in Robert DeMoss, *Sex and the Single Person* (Grand Rapids, Mich.: Zondervan, 1995), p. 37.

[45]Collins, *Christian Counseling,* p. 365.

Chapter 2: A Brief History of Singleness

[1]Cited in Ruth Tucker, *The Family Album* (Wheaton, Ill.: Victor, 1994), p. 80.

[2]Nancy Hardesty, "Being Single in Today's World," in Gary Collins, ed., *It's O.K. to Be Single* (Waco, Tex.: Word, 1976), p. 15.

[3]Rodney Clapp, *Families at the Crossroads* (Downers Grove, Ill.: InterVarsity Press, 1993), p. 95.

[4]Ibid., p. 97.

[5]Henry C. Lea, *The History of Sacerdotal Celibacy in the Christian Church* (New York: Russell & Russell, 1957), p. 4.

[6]Rabbi Eleazar, in the Talmud, *Yeb.* 63a; cited in Leon Morris, *The First Epistle of Paul to the Corinthians* (Grand Rapids, Mich.: Eerdmans, 1985), p. 104.

[7]Raba and Rabbi Ishmael, Talmud, *Kidd.* 29b; cited in Morris, *First Epistle of Paul to the Corinthians*, p. 104.

[8]Craig Blomberg writes, "The ultimate destiny of redeemed humanity is life in community, with all believers sharing a kind of intimacy that is even better than what spouses experience with each other in the marriage relationship. We believe, following Jesus' teaching, that in the life to come we, like angels, will not be sexually active beings (Mt 22:30). We do not hold this belief because we consider sex evil (as certain forms of traditional Catholicism often did), but because we assume that the relationships all Christians will have with each other will make the excitement of sex pale in comparison!" (Craig Blomberg and Stephen Robinson, *How Wide the Divide?* [Downers Grove, Ill.: InterVarsity Press, 1997], p. 104.)

[9]Robert L. Stern, "How Priests Came to Be Celibate: An Oversimplification," in *Celibacy in the Church*, ed. William W. Bassett and Peter Huizing (New York: Herder and Herder, 1972), p. 77.

[10]Stanley Grenz, *Sexual Ethics* (Waco, Tex.: Word, 1990), p. 165.

[11]V. M. Sinton, "Singleness," in *New Dictionary of Christian Ethics & Pastoral Theology*, ed. David J. Atkinson, David F. Field, Arthur Holmes and Oliver O'Donovan (Downers Grove, Ill.: InterVarsity Press, 1995), p. 791.

[12]Lea, *History of Sacerdotal Celibacy*, pp. 14-15.

[13]Philip Schaff, *History of the Christian Church* (Grand Rapids, Mich.: Eerdmans, 1979), II, 788, cited in Tucker, *Family Album*, p. 79.

[14]Elaine Pagels, *Adam, Eve and the Serpent* (New York: Random House, 1988), p. 80.

[15]Rebecca Harden Weaver, "Yes, But . . .: Early Christian Teaching on Marriage, Sex, and Family," *Regeneration Quarterly* 1 (Summer 1995): 28.

[16]Ibid.

[17]Cited in Henry Bettenson, ed., *Documents of the Christian Church*, 2nd ed. (London: Oxford University Press, 1963), p. 35.

[18]Cited in Weaver, "Yes, But . . .," p. 27.

[19]Cited in Pagels, *Adam, Eve and the Serpent*, pp. 94-95. Pagels mentions other early church perspectives on the topic, such as Methodius, who wrote a famous polemic titled *Symposium of the Ten Virgins*, in which ten women ascetics compete with each other in praising virginity. In this discourse marriage is described as something of a necessary evil to multiply the human race, but only to the end of producing the true human being, the celibate. One of the women, Thaelia, admits that Paul did not *require* celibacy, but she is certain that he preferred it for any who were capable of achieving this "means of restoring humanity to Paradise" (pp. 85-86).

[20]Cited in Clapp, *Families at the Crossroads*, p. 93.

[21]Will Durant, *The Age of Faith* (New York: Simon & Schuster, 1950), p. 45.

[22]P. Delhaye, "Celibacy, History of," in *New Catholic Encyclopedia* (New York: McGraw Hill, 1967). Also, Will Durant summarizes, "In reaction against the sexual license of pagan morals, some Christian enthusiasts concluded from a passage in St. Paul [1 Cor 7:32] that any commerce between the sexes was sinful; they denounced all marriage, and trembled at the abomination of a married priest. The provincial council of Gengra (c. 362) condemned these views as heretical, but the Church increasingly demanded celibacy in her priests. . . . A Roman synod of 386 advised the complete continence of the clergy; and a year later Pope Siricius ordered the unfrocking of any priest who married, or continued to live with his wife. Jerome, Ambrose and Augustine supported this decree with their triple power; and after a generation of sporadic resistance it was enforced with transient success in the West." In Durant, *Age of Faith*, p. 45.

[23]Throughout the Middle Ages, the church defended clerical celibacy "on the ground that a married priest, consciously or not, would put his loyalty to wife and children above his devotion to the Church; that for their sake he would be tempted to accumulate money or property; that he would try to transmit his see or benefice to one of his offspring; that an hereditary ecclesiastical caste might in this way develop in Europe as in India; and that the combined economic power of such a propertied priesthood would be too great for the papacy to control. The priest should be totally devoted to God, the Church and his fellow men." In Durant, *Age of Faith*, p. 542.

[24]Pope John Paul II, *Apostolic Exhortation of His Holiness: The Role of the Christian Family in the Modern World* (St. Paul Editions, 1981), pp. 29-30, cited in Paul Stevens, *Marriage Spirituality* (Downers Grove, Ill.: InterVarsity Press, 1989), pp. 110-11.

[25]Lea, *History of Sacerdotal Celibacy*, p. 22.

[26]The Creed had previously said that the Spirit proceeds from the Father. The church later added *filioque*, which means "and the Son" in Latin, so that the Creed then stated that the Spirit proceeds from both the Father and the Son. Orthodox hold that this contradicts John 15:26.

[27]Durant, *Age of Faith*, p. 544.

[28]Will Durant, *The Reformation* (New York: Simon & Schuster, 1957), p. 21.

[29]Ibid.

[30]Cited in Tucker, *Family Album*, p. 110.

[31]Cited in Heiko A. Oberman, *Luther: Man Between God and the Devil* (New York: Image/Doubleday, 1992), p. 272.

[32]Ibid., p. 111.

[33]Ibid., p. 110.

[34]Cited in Harold Ivan Smith, "The Church's History of Marriage, Divorce, Remarriage and Singleness," in *Singles Ministry Handbook*, ed. Douglas L. Fagerstrom (Wheaton, Ill.: Victor, 1988), p. 21.

[35]Tucker, *Family Album*, p. 112.

[36]Smith, "Church's History," *Singles Ministry Handbook*, p. 21.

[37]Cited in Oberman, *Luther*, pp. 275-76.

[38]Ibid., p. 282.

[39]Smith, "Church's History," *Singles Ministry Handbook*, p. 22.

[40]Ibid.

[41]For a critique of modern evangelical "family theology" and a historical trace of the roots of the nuclear family, see Rodney Clapp's *Families at the Crossroads* (Downers Grove, Ill.: InterVarsity Press, 1993).

[42]Justo Gonzalez, *The Story of Christianity,* vol. 2 (San Francisco: Harper San Francisco, 1985), p. 241.

[43]Ruth Tucker, *Women in the Maze* (Downers Grove, Ill.: InterVarsity Press, 1992), p. 180.

[44]Ibid., p. 239.

[45]Ibid., pp. 236-37.

Chapter 3: The Myth of the Gift

[1]C. Peter Wagner, *Your Spiritual Gifts Can Help Your Church Grow,* rev. ed. (Ventura, Calif.: Regal, 1994), p. 57.

[2]Smith, *Should I Get Married?* p. 27.

[3]Simon J. Kistemaker, *New Testament Commentary: Exposition of the First Epistle to the Corinthians* (Grand Rapids, Mich.: Baker, 1993), p. 215.

[4]F. W. Grosheide, *Commentary on the First Epistle to the Corinthians* (Grand Rapids, Mich.: Eerdmans, 1953), p. 159.

[5]J. Mack Stiles, *Speaking of Jesus* (Downers Grove, Ill.: InterVarsity Press, 1995), pp. 112-13.

[6]Tim Stafford, *Sexual Chaos* (Downers Grove, Ill.: InterVarsity Press, 1993), p. 146.

[7]Gordon D. Fee, *The First Epistle to the Corinthians* (Grand Rapids, Mich.: Eerdmans, 1987), p. 285.

[8]John Howard Yoder, *Singleness in Ethical and Pastoral Perspective* (Elkhart, Ind.: Associated Mennonite Biblical Seminaries, 1974), p. 2.

[9]Collins, *Christian Counseling,* p. 361.

[10]Kistemaker, *First Epistle to the Corinthians,* pp. 214-15.

[11]Oswald Chambers, *My Utmost for His Highest,* updated ed. (Grand Rapids, Mich.: Discovery House, 1995), January 26 entry.

[12]Clapp, *Families at the Crossroads,* p. 112.

[13]Walter Trobisch, *Love Is a Feeling to Be Learned* (Downers Grove, Ill.: InterVarsity Press, 1971), p. 18.

[14]Robert Hicks, *Uneasy Manhood* (Nashville: Nelson, 1991), p. 78.

[15]Paul Tournier, *The Adventure of Living* (New York: Harper & Row, 1965), p. 135.

[16]Trobisch, *Love Is a Feeling to Be Learned,* p. 18.

[17]J. E. O'Day, *Discovering Your Spiritual Gifts* (Downers Grove, Ill.: InterVarsity Press, 1985).

[18]F. Godet, *Commentary on St. Paul's First Epistle to the Corinthians* (T & T Clark, 1889), I, 328, cited in David Prior, *The Message of 1 Corinthians* (Downers Grove, Ill.: InterVarsity Press, 1985), p. 120.

[19]Grenz, *Sexual Ethics,* p. 163.

Chapter 4: The Issue of God's Will

[1]For the view that God's will is not specific to each individual, see Garry Friesen with J. Robin Maxon, *Decision Making and the Will of God* (Portland, Ore.: Multnomah, 1980). For the view that God has a best will for each person and it is our responsibility to freely follow and choose that will, see M. Blaine Smith, *Knowing God's Will,* rev. ed. (Downers Grove, Ill.: InterVarsity Press, 1991).

[2]Smith, *Knowing God's Will,* pp. 48-49.

[3]Bill Hybels, *Too Busy Not to Pray* (Downers Grove, Ill.: InterVarsity Press, 1988), p. 107. (See especially chapters 10-12 for suggestions for hearing God's leadings in prayer.)

[4]Paul Little suggests a similar formula in his booklet *Affirming the Will of God* (Downers Grove, Ill.: InterVarsity Press, 1971). His four principles of guidance are the Word of God,

prayer, circumstances and the counsel of other Christians.

[5]J. I. Packer, *Knowing God*, rev. ed. (Downers Grove, Ill.: InterVarsity Press, 1993), pp. 235-36.

[6]John Stott, *Your Mind Matters* (Downers Grove, Ill.: InterVarsity Press, 1972), pp. 44-45.

[7]Friesen, *Decision Making*, p. 298.

[8]Stafford, *Sexual Chaos*, p. 141.

[9]J. Allan Petersen, *The Myth of the Greener Grass*, rev. ed. (Wheaton, Ill.: Tyndale House, 1991), p. 60.

[10]Rick Stedman, *Pure Joy: The Positive Side of Single Sexuality* (Chicago: Moody, 1993), p. 180.

[11]Smith, *Should I Get Married?* p. 35.

[12]Diane Ackerman, *A Natural History of Love* (New York: Vintage Books, 1994), pp. 74, 97.

[13]Ibid., pp. 95-96. For Hollywood's version of this concept, see the 1991 film *The Butcher's Wife*, starring Demi Moore and Jeff Daniels. Demi Moore's character believes that each person has a "split-apart," the missing half each is destined to find. She uses this belief to justify leaving her husband to find her "split-apart."

[14]Smith, *Should I Get Married?* pp. 34, 38.

[15]Petersen, *The Myth of the Greener Grass*, pp. 60-61.

[16]Stedman, *Pure Joy*, p. 180.

[17]Smith, *Should I Get Married?* p. 36.

[18]Petersen, *The Myth of the Greener Grass*, p. 61.

[19]Smith, *Should I Get Married?* p. 36.

[20]Daniel Taylor, "Two Good to be True," *Moody*, February 1991, p. 17.

[21]Stedman, *Pure Joy*, p. 180.

[22]Bruce Reichenbach, "God Limits His Power," in *Predestination and Free Will*, ed. David Basinger and Randall Basinger, (Downers Grove, Ill.: InterVarsity Press, 1986), pp. 106-7.

[23]Exodus 4:21; 7:3; 9:12; 10:1, 20, 27; 11:10; 14:4, 8, 17 say that God is the subject of the verb *to harden*. Exodus 7:13, 14, 22; 8:15, 19, 32; 9:7, 34-35; 13:15 say that Pharaoh hardened his own heart. It is suggested that God in his foreknowledge knew that Pharaoh would harden his heart, and so God made an initial prediction that at some later point in time, God would harden Pharaoh's heart. But from Pharaoh's point of view, he hardened his own heart against Moses. Only after a repeated pattern of Pharaoh's stubbornness—not until the sixth plague—did God actually do the hardening. This seems to indicate that God lets us go our own way to some point of no return, at which point he gives us over to our sin (see Rom 1:24-28). See Walter C. Kaiser Jr., *Toward Old Testament Ethics* (Grand Rapids, Mich.: Zondervan, 1983), pp. 252-56.

[24]William Coleman, *Cupid Is Stupid!* (Downers Grove, Ill.: InterVarsity Press, 1991), p. 66.

[25]Tournier, *Adventure of Living*, p. 138.

[26]Collins, *Christian Counseling*, p. 369.

[27]"A HIS Interview with John R. W. Stott," *HIS* (October 1975), p. 19.

[28]See the appendix for the complete transcript of this interview. Note that Stott and I disagree slightly on our views of singleness. He equates a special call to singleness with the gift of singleness, while I do not. He also says "marriage is the norm, singleness the abnorm," which I feel is an overstatement. I would prefer to say that, culturally, marriage tends to be the norm and singleness tends to be the exception.

[29]An example of this is found in Laura Esquivel's novel *Like Water For Chocolate* (New York: Doubleday, 1992). Tita, the youngest daughter, falls in love with Pedro, but she is not permitted to marry him because she is obligated to remain at home and take care of her widowed mother. Pedro then marries Tita's older sister in order to stay close to her. It is only

after the death of her mother that Tita is free to marry.

[30]Friesen, *Decision-Making,* p. 289.

[31]Yoder, *Singleness,* p. 2.

[32]Grenz, *Sexual Ethics,* p. 166.

[33]Ed Young, *Romancing the Home* (Nashville: Broadman and Holman, 1994), p. 41.

[34]Friesen, *Decision Making,* p. 287.

Chapter 5: Freedom and Opportunity

[1]Mary Fisher notes that "unmarried people can define themselves far more easily as a child of the kingdom of God than as an Australian, an American or a Chinese person. People who raise young children face the challenge of passing on who they are within terms of their nationality and roots. . . . But an unmarried person doesn't have to worry about the issue of nationality so much." In "An interview on singleness with Urbana 93 Associate Director Mary Fisher," *Options in Action* newsletter, No. 5, InterVarsity Christian Fellowship, p. 2.

[2]Clapp, *Families at the Crossroads,* p. 101.

[3]Stafford, *Sexual Chaos,* p. 151.

[4]Clapp, *Families at the Crossroads,* p. 100.

[5]Richard Foster, *The Freedom of Simplicity* (San Francisco: HarperSan Francisco, 1981), p. 136.

[6]Ibid.

[7]Stott, interview with the author.

[8]Stafford, *Sexual Chaos,* p. 150.

[9]Hicks, *Uneasy Manhood,* p. 96.

[10]Ibid., p. 97.

[11]William Hendriksen, *New Testament Commentary: Exposition of the Pastoral Epistles* (Grand Rapids, Mich.: Baker, 1957), p. 121.

[12]Dan Harrison and Gordon Aeschliman, *Romancing the Globe: The Call of the Wild on Generation X* (Downers Grove, Ill.: InterVarsity Press, 1993), pp. 13-16.

[13]Stanley J. Grenz and Roy D. Bell, *Betrayal of Trust* (Downers Grove, Ill.: InterVarsity Press, 1995), pp. 71-72.

[14]Grenz, *Sexual Ethics,* p. 172.

[15]"The Booklist Interview," *Booklist,* October 1, 1996, pp. 302-3.

[16]Kathleen Norris, *The Cloister Walk* (New York: Riverhead Books, 1996), pp. 260-62.

[17]Ibid., pp. 255, 260, 262.

[18]Stafford, *Sexual Chaos,* pp. 150-51.

[19]See Albert Hsu, "The Dilbertization of America: Re-envisioning work in the age of the cubicle," *Regeneration Quarterly* 2 (Winter 1996): 5.

[20]George Barna, *Baby Busters: The Disillusioned Generation* (Chicago: Northfield/Moody, 1994), p. 37.

[21]Tim Celek and Dieter Zander, *Inside the Soul of a New Generation* (Grand Rapids, Mich.: Zondervan, 1996), p. 33.

[22]Coupland, *Generation X,* p. 35.

[23]Outlook, *U.S. News and World Report,* October 16, 1995, p. 12.

[24]Judith Allen Shelly, *Not Just a Job* (Downers Grove, Ill.: InterVarsity Press, 1985), p. 75.

[25]Smith, *Should I Get Married?* pp. 83-84.

[26]Warren, *Finding the Love of Your Life,* p. 63.

[27]Ibid., p. 11.

[28]Mary Franzen Clark, *Hiding, Hurting, Healing* (Grand Rapids, Mich.: Zondervan, 1985), pp.

90-91.

[29]Tournier, *Adventure of Living,* p. 135.

[30]Clapp, *Families at the Crossroads,* pp. 106-7.

[31]Yoder, *Singleness,* p. 4.

[32]Collins, *Christian Counseling,* p. 364.

[33]Koons and Anthony, *Single Adult Passages,* p. 87.

[34]Ibid., p. 88.

[35]Yoder, *Singleness,* p. 6.

[36]Foster, *Freedom of Simplicity,* p. 137.

Chapter 6: From Loneliness to Solitude

[1]Michael Curtis and Greg Mains, "The One Where Heckles Dies," Kevin Bright (director), *Friends,* October 5, 1995, NBC.

[2]I am here referring only to physical aloneness, not to the generational aloneness of *feeling* alone characterized by Tim Celek and Dieter Zander: "Feeling alone is different from feeling lonely. Loneliness is the experience of having no one around with whom to connect. Aloneness is the experience of being in a crowd and being unable to connect with people in a deeply fulfilling manner." Celek and Zander, *Inside the Soul of a New Generation,* p. 25. See chapter 7 for a discussion of different levels of aloneness.

[3]Barbara Sroka, *One Is a Whole Number* (Wheaton, Ill.: Victor, 1978), p. 30.

[4]Helena Wilkinson, *Beyond Singleness* (London: Marshall Pickering, 1995), p. 7.

[5]Richard Foster, *Celebration of Discipline,* rev. ed. (San Francisco: HarperSanFrancisco, 1988), p. 96.

[6]Wilkinson, *Beyond Singleness,* p. 9.

[7]Gerald Sittser, *A Grace Disguised* (Grand Rapids, Mich.: Zondervan, 1996), pp. 111-12.

[8]Coupland, *Generation X,* p. 27.

[9]Walter Wangerin Jr., *Mourning into Dancing* (Grand Rapids, Mich.: Zondervan, 1992), pp. 91-92.

[10]Collins, *Christian Counseling,* p. 369.

[11]Clifford E. Bajema, *The Discipline of Meditation and the Practice of Holiness* (Madison, Wisc.: published by the author, 1994), p. 75.

[12]Ibid., pp. 75-76.

[13]Richard Foster, *Prayer: Finding the Heart's True Home* (San Francisco: HarperSanFrancisco, 1992), pp. 50-51.

[14]Foster, *Prayer,* p. 53.

[15]Ibid., p. 54.

[16]Margaret Clarkson, *So You're Single!* (Wheaton, Ill.: Harold Shaw, 1978), p. 81.

[17]Trobisch, *Love Is a Feeling to Be Learned,* p. 18.

[18]Ibid.

[19]Stafford, *Sexual Chaos,* p. 141.

[20]In Elisabeth Elliot, *Shadow of the Almighty* (San Francisco: HarperSanFrancisco, 1958), pp. 212-13.

[21]Henri Nouwen, *The Way of the Heart* (San Francisco: HarperSanFrancisco, 1981), pp. 26-27.

[22]Henri Nouwen, *Reaching Out* (New York: Doubleday, 1975), p. 25.

[23]Foster, *Celebration of Discipline,* p. 96.

[24]Dallas Willard, *The Spirit of the Disciplines* (San Francisco: Harper & Row, 1988), p. 160.

[25]Nouwen, *Way of the Heart,* p. 27.

[26]Foster, *Celebration of Discipline*, p. 96.

[27]Nouwen, *Way of the Heart*, p. 34.

[28]Ibid., p. 39.

Chapter 7: From Aloneness to Community

[1]Tim LaHaye and Jerry Jenkins, *Left Behind* (Wheaton, Ill.: Tyndale House, 1995).

[2]Tim LaHaye and Jerry Jenkins, *Tribulation Force* (Wheaton, Ill.: Tyndale House, 1996), pp. 129, 157.

[3]If anything, this contradicts statements in Scripture that seem to suggest that singles are more capable of enduring tribulation than those who are married. Paul's guidance in 1 Corinthians 7:26-27 is, "Because of the present crisis, I think that it is good for you to remain as you are. . . . Are you unmarried? Do not look for a wife." While commentators are divided over the nature of the "present crisis" and Paul's warning that "the time is short" (v. 29), a distinct possibility is that Paul's admonitions are especially applicable in light of Christ's impending return. Therefore, these characters really had no business getting married.

[4]U.S. Bureau of the Census, in Famighetti, *World Almanac 1995*, pp. 961, 373; see also Arlene F. Saluter, "Marital Status and Living Arrangements," U.S. Bureau of the Census, *Population Profile of the United States: 1995* (Washington: U.S. Government Printing Office, 1995).

[5]Sue Grafton's detective heroine, Kinsey Millhone, articulates it this way: "Being single can be confusing. On the one hand, you sometimes yearn for the simple comfort of companionship; someone to discuss your day with, someone with whom you can celebrate a raise or tax refund, someone who'll commiserate when you're down with a cold. On the other hand, once you get used to being alone (in other words, having everything your way), you have to wonder why you'd ever take on the aggravation of a relationship. Other human beings have all these hotly held *opinions*, habits, and mannerisms, bad art and peculiar taste in music, not to mention mood disorders, food preferences, passions, hobbies, allergies, emotional fixations, and attitudes that in no way coincide with the correct ones, namely yours." In Sue Grafton, *"M" Is for Malice* (New York: Henry Holt, 1996), p. 42.

[6]"Voices from Cyberspace: Generation Xers in their Own Words," *WCA Monthly*, September-October 1995.

[7]Janet Bernardi and William Mahedy, *A Generation Alone: Xers Making a Place in the World* (Downers Grove, Ill.: InterVarsity Press, 1994), p. 20.

[8]Ibid., p. 21.

[9]Coupland, *Generation X*, p. 69.

[10]Bernardi and Mahedy, *Generation Alone*, p. 20.

[11]Ibid., p. 21.

[12]Frank G. Kirkpatrick, *Community: A Trinity of Models* (Washington, D.C.: Georgetown University Press, 1986), p. 52.

[13]Kathy O'Malley, "Friends Chicago Style," *Chicago Tribune*, Sept. 21, 1995, section 5, p. 2.

[14]J. Oswald Sanders, "Lonely But Never Alone," booklet published by Radio Bible Class (Grand Rapids, Mich., 1991), excerpted from J. Oswald Sanders, *Facing Loneliness: The Starting Point of a New Journey* (Grand Rapids, Mich.: Discovery House, 1991).

[15]Nouwen, *Reaching Out*, pp. 29-30.

[16]Clapp, *Families at the Crossroads*, pp. 67-68.

[17]Ibid., p. 74.

[18]Cited in Bettenson, *Documents of the Christian Church*, p. 73.

[19]Grenz, *Sexual Ethics*, p. 168.

[20]Gary McIntosh and Glen Martin, *Finding Them, Keeping Them* (Nashville: Broadman, 1992), p. 47.

[21]Richard Foster, "Becoming Like Christ," *Christianity Today*, February 5, 1996, p. 28.

[22]Rodney Clapp, "Is the 'Traditional Family' Biblical?" *Christianity Today*, September 16, 1988, p. 25.

[23]Clapp, *Families at the Crossroads*, pp. 76-77.

[24]Lyle Schaller, *Assimilating New Members* (Nashville: Abingdon, 1978), p. 82.

[25]Collins, *Christian Counseling*, pp. 362, 372.

[26]**Kairos's Vision Statement**

Kairos is a Christian community of single adults committed to encouraging one another to lead obedient, fulfilling lives as followers of Jesus Christ.

To accomplish this, Kairos is committed to these values:

1. *Spiritual Growth.* We advocate the practice of spiritual disciplines, such as prayer, Bible study, and worship, so that we may continually grow in our relationship with God, becoming more Christlike and mature in behavior and attitude.

2. *Community.* As the body of Christ, our intent is to develop a community that embodies God's desire for healthy interpersonal relationships, facilitating fellowship and demonstrating by example Christian love for one another.

3. *Discipleship.* Because Jesus calls us to be his disciples and to disciple one another, we invest in the lives of all members of our group, challenging one another to greater faith and accountability in our walk with Christ.

4. *Hospitality.* Recognizing that God values individuals of all backgrounds, we desire that our community welcome newcomers, be sensitive to their concerns, and provide opportunities for visitors to find a place to belong.

5. *Teaching.* Convinced of the authority of Scripture, we are committed to regular study, understanding and practical application of the Word of God, through relevant and biblical class lessons and small group Bible studies.

6. *Service.* With Jesus' servant leadership as our model, we encourage one another to serve God in kingdom-strategic ways, using our spiritual gifts to impact the lives of other people in our church, our community and our world.

7. *Evangelism.* In order to participate in the work of the Great Commission, we intentionally develop an outreach worldview, sharing the good news of Jesus and inviting others into the kingdom of God on both a local and global level.

In all of our activities, we support the ministry and vision statement of Blanchard Road Alliance Church: *As God's family, we want to worship Him well in all we do, develop people by building disciples, and grow by reaching people outside His family.*

[27]Jim Smoke, "Building Community in a Singles Ministry," in *Singles Ministry Handbook*, ed. Douglas Fagerstrom (Wheaton, Ill.: Victor, 1988), p. 200.

[28]Stafford, *Sexual Chaos*, p. 163.

[29]Richard Lamb, *Following Jesus in the "Real World"* (Downers Grove, Ill.: InterVarsity Press, 1995), pp. 94-113.

[30]Bernardi and Mahedy, *A Generation Alone*, p. 74.

[31]Johnson, "Singleness and Sexuality."

[32]See Clapp, "Is the 'Traditional Family' Biblical?" and *Families at the Crossroads*, p. 107. Also see Mary Stewart Van Leeuwen, *Gender and Grace* (Downers Grove, Ill.: InterVarsity Press,

1990), p. 176.

[33]Pepper Schwartz, "Children's New Bonds: Para-Dads, Para-Moms," *The New York Times*, Nov. 9, 1995, B1.

[34]Stott, interview with the author.

[35]Gary L. McIntosh, *Three Generations* (Grand Rapids, Mich.: Revell, 1995), p. 145.

[36]Clapp, *Families at the Crossroads*, p. 78.

Chapter 8: Rethinking Romance

[1]Anne Tyler, *Breathing Lessons* (New York: Berkley Books, 1988), p. 67.

[2]Clapp, "Why Christians Have Lousy Sex Lives," *Regeneration Quarterly* 1 (Summer 1995): 7.

[3]Douglas Coupland, *Microserfs* (New York: ReganBooks/Harper Collins, 1995), p. 291.

[4]Yoder, *Singleness*, p. 5.

[5]Clapp, "Why Christians Have Lousy Sex Lives," p. 9.

[6]Jon Hassler, *Simon's Night* (New York: Ballantine, 1979), p. 206.

[7]Yoder, *Singleness*, p. 4.

[8]Clapp, "Why Christians Have Lousy Sex Lives," p. 8.

[9]Jack Balswick, *Men at the Crossroads* (Downers Grove, Ill.: InterVarsity Press, 1992), p. 194.

[10]Oberman, *Luther*, p. 281.

[11]Ibid., p. 280.

[12]Even in marriages that weren't arranged per se, in the Bible romantic love often took a back seat to other concerns. For example, Christians often read the story of Ruth and Boaz as a romantic love story. But this is to read our Western bias into the text. Though it may seem cynical, a plain reading of the story seems to indicate that Ruth and Naomi were more concerned about finding a home and provision for Ruth than finding true love (3:1), and they took (perhaps manipulative) steps to get Boaz to marry Ruth. Furthermore, nowhere in the entire book of Ruth does it actually say that Ruth and Boaz loved each other. The only person Ruth is mentioned as loving is her mother-in-law, Naomi.

[13]Robert Fulghum, *Maybe (Maybe Not)* (New York: Villard Books, 1993), pp. 172-73.

[14]Stott, interview with the author.

[15]Hybels and Wilkins, *Tender Love*, p. 132.

[16]Bill and Lynne Hybels, *Fit to Be Tied* (Grand Rapids, Mich.: Zondervan, 1991), p. 83.

[17]Clapp, "Why Christians Have Lousy Sex Lives," p. 9.

[18]Rodney Clapp, "Why the Devil Takes Visa: A Christian response to the triumph of consumerism," *Christianity Today*, October 7, 1996, p. 29.

[19]Ibid. Clapp continues, "In the Christian way, lifetime monogamy makes sense. In the consumer way of life, serial monogamy (a succession of mates, one at a time) is a much more sensible practice. Highly increased divorce rates signal many things, but one of them surely is that consumption is our way of life."

[20]Clapp, *Families at the Crossroads*, pp. 109-10.

[21]Leith Anderson, *Dying for Change*, pp. 106-7.

[22]Celek and Zander, *Inside the Soul of a New Generation*, p. 106.

[23]Alice and Robert Fryling, *A Handbook for Engaged Couples*, rev. ed. (Downers Grove, Ill.: InterVarsity Press, 1996).

[24]Keith Anderson, *Is This the One?* (Downers Grove, Ill.: InterVarsity Press, 1996), p. 22.

[25]Some good places to start are *Making Friends and Making Them Count* by Em Griffin, *True Love in a World of False Hope* by Robbie Castleman, *Dating, Sex and Friendship* by Joyce Huggett, *Overcoming Shyness* by M. Blaine Smith and *Friendships That Run Deep* by Keith

Anderson (all IVP).

[26]Stafford, *Sexual Chaos*, p. 150.

[27]Grenz and Bell, *Betrayal of Trust*, p. 80.

[28]Tom L. Eisenman, *Temptations Men Face* (Downers Grove, Ill.: InterVarsity Press, 1990), p. 63.

[29]Mary Ellen Ashcroft, *Temptations Women Face* (Downers Grove, Ill.: InterVarsity Press, 1991), p. 119.

[30]Francine Rivers, "Hooked on Romance," *Today's Christian Woman*, May-June 1995, p. 40.

[31]DeMoss, *Sex and Single Person*, p. 27.

[32]Stott, interview with the author.

[33]Paul K. Jewett, *Man as Male and Female* (Grand Rapids, Mich.: Eerdmans, 1975), p. 110.

[34]Clapp, *Families at the Crossroads*, p. 106.

[35]Foster, *Celebration of Discipline*, p. 43.

[36]"The War Within: An Anatomy of Lust," *Leadership*, Fall 1982, pp. 42-43.

[37]Foster, *Celebration of Discipline*, pp. 4-5.

[38]Kathleen Norris, *The Cloister Walk* (New York: Riverhead Books, 1996), p. 118.

[39]Ibid., p. 261.

[40]Ibid., p. 120.

[41]Ibid., p. 118.

[42]Ibid., p. 117.

[43]Ibid., p. 254.

[44]Ibid.

[45]Ibid., p. 263.

[46]Ibid., p. 256.

[47]Ibid., p. 260.

[48]Ibid., p. 263.

[49]Hobart Mowrer, *Learning Theory and Personality Dynamics* (New York: Ronald Press, 1950), p. 601, cited in Robert Webber, *God Still Speaks* (Nashville: Nelson, 1980), p. 180.

Chapter 9: Temptations Singles Face

[1]Anne Tyler, *The Accidental Tourist* (New York: Berkley Books, 1985), p. 121.

[2]Collins, *Christian Counseling*, p. 372.

[3]Elisa Morgan, *I'm Tired of Waiting!* (Wheaton, Ill.: Victor, 1989), p. 49.

[4]Henry David Thoreau, *Walden*, in *Major American Writers*, ed. Howard Mumford Jones, Ernest E. Leisy and Richard M. Ludwig, 3rd ed.(New York: Harcourt Brace, 1952), p. 914.

[5]Charles Hummel, *Tyranny of the Urgent*, rev. ed. (Downers Grove, Ill.: InterVarsity Press, 1994). Also see his new book, *Freedom from Tyranny of the Urgent* (Downers Grove, Ill.: InterVarsity Press, 1997).

[6]Stott, interview with the author.

[7]Larry Burkett, *Investing for the Future* calendar (Wheaton, Ill.: Victor, 1993), March 1 entry.

[8]Patrick Johnstone, *Operation World*, 5th ed. (Grand Rapids, Mich.: Zondervan, 1993), p. 395.

[9]Rod Handley suggests these questions in his book *Character Counts* (Grand Island, Nebr.: Cross Training, 1995):

Have you spent daily time in Scripture and prayer?

Have you had any flirtatious or lustful attitudes, tempting thoughts, or exposed yourself to any explicit materials that would not glorify God?

Have you been completely above reproach in your financial dealings?

Have you spent quality relationship time with your family and friends?

Have you done your 100% best in your job or school?

Have you told any half-truths or outright lies, putting yourself in a better light to those around you?

Have you shared the gospel with an unbeliever this week?

Have you taken care of your body through daily physical exercise and proper eating and sleeping habits?

Have you allowed any person or circumstances to rob you of your joy?

Did you just lie about any of your answers?

[10]Sue Grafton, *"E" Is for Evidence* (New York: Bantam, 1988), p. 3.

[11]Abigail Van Buren, "Dear Abby" syndicated column, February 5, 1995.

[12]Tournier, *Adventure of Living,* p. 138.

Epilogue: A Vision for the Future
[1]Philip Friedman, *Inadmissible Evidence* (New York: Ivy/Ballantine, 1992), p. 629.

[2]Clapp, "Is the 'Traditional Family' Biblical?" p. 27.

[3]Stafford, *Sexual Chaos,* p. 147.

[4]Hybels and Hybels, *Fit to Be Tied,* p. 29.